A Father is Born by Tumiso Mashaba is a gripping, poetic, vivid, and deeply entertaining memoir that cracks open new vistas on identity, love, friendship, memory and dislocation. It demonstrates Mashaba's brilliance in exploring the complex moral issues and secret interconnections of human relations in a compelling way.
– Niq Mhlongo, author

Tumiso's simple yet eloquently written personal memoir tells a story of grief and pain, but also of triumph and freedom. With such an uneasy journey through life, someone else would have chosen to wallow in self-pity and blame everything on everyone else. Not him. The courage of conviction he displays in this book – wearing his scars like medals, even when he exposes his own vulnerability – is something to behold. – Vuyo Mvoko, journalist

A Father is Born

TUMISO MASHABA

A Memoir

Jonathan Ball Publishers
Johannesburg · Cape Town · London

All rights reserved.
No part of this publication may be reproduced or transmitted,
in any form or by any means, without prior permission
from the publisher or copyright holder.

© Text, Tumiso Mashaba 2021
© Published edition, 2021 Jonathan Ball Publishers

Originally published in South Africa in 2021 by
JONATHAN BALL PUBLISHERS
A division of Media24 (Pty) Ltd
PO Box 33977
Jeppestown
2043

ISBN 978-1-77619-124-6
eBook ISBN 978-1-77619-125-3

Every effort has been made to trace the copyright holders and to obtain their permission for the use of copyright material. The publishers apologise for any errors or omissions and would be grateful to be notified of any corrections that should be incorporated in future editions of this book.

Website: www.jonathanball.co.za
Twitter: www.twitter.com/JonathanBallPub
Facebook: www.facebook.com/JonathanBallPublishers

Cover by publicide
Design and typesetting by Catherine Coetzer
Set in PT Serif

To Synové, Imani and Neo

Contents

PROLOGUE ix

PART ONE
1 Mirror 15
2 'O mang? Wa ga mang?' – 'Who are you? Whose child are you?' 27
3 First born third 38
4 A father is born 48

PART TWO
5 Curious wonder 67
6 The strange man 79
7 Tshepo 94

PART THREE
8 Picking up the pieces – Part 1 107
9 Life lessons 121
10 As fragile as an egg 138
11 A family gathering 152

PART FOUR

12	The possibility of just being ...	167
13	A long way from home	176
14	Great expectations	187
15	Synové (A gift from the sun)	194
16	Picking up the pieces – Part 2	203
17	Imani (Faith)	214
18	Making a home	226
19	Neo (A gift)	239

EPILOGUE	247
ABOUT THE AUTHOR	251

Prologue

Our physical scars lie on the surface where the naked eye can see them. We conceal them with make-up. We massage them at night with tissue oil in the hope they will appear less prominent one day. They are visible reminders of what we've been through in life, what dangers we've escaped. They are testament to our imperfections, our flaws and our failings.

I got the scar on my right cheek when I was around six years old. We had just gotten off a taxi, my folks and me. I think we were coming back from my crèche graduation ceremony. I was super-excited and I just ran ahead of my parents without looking. My father tried to slow me down, but I wouldn't listen.

I don't know if I tripped, but I missed my step and the next thing I knew I went crashing down into a barbed wired fence. I fell, and it was lights out. A moment later, when I came to, I was in my father's arms, bleeding from a deep gash on my right cheek. I cried all the way home. My parents applied some Mercurochrome and the following day I was out playing again. A week later it was fully healed. But I was left with an unmistakeable scar on my right cheek.

The scar, although still visible, has somewhat faded over the years. It's a facial fixture that I've had to live with. It wasn't a deep scar, but the barbed wired fence decisively etched its memory onto my face. I've been called 'scar face' because of it. I've hated it. I've loathed looking at myself in the mirror because of it. I've learnt to just ignore it. I've learnt to embrace it. I've learnt to love it and at one point in my life I even forgot about it.

But some scars aren't as forgettable. Some really cut deep, deep into one's soul. They are not visible to the naked eye. They are difficult to define and mind-numbing to comprehend. They could lie dormant for years only to be triggered by something as banal as the scent of a cologne. Or it could be an old photograph stumbling out of a bookshelf that has you reliving, in an instant, what you thought you had long erased from your life. These scars could take you over, enveloping you in a state of perpetual pain, shame and self-condemnation. Alcohol can become the temporary fix for those impalpable wounds, or it could be the bedsides of many different lovers that are the morphine that numbs the pain.

It's usually the ones closest to us that are responsible for delivering these invisible blows. In my case, it was my late father, Neo 'Snowy' Mashaba. It took me years to realise how much of an adverse effect my relationship with my father had on me. How I think. How I reason. How I process things. How I feel. How I react. How I relate to others. How I love, even. All pointed back to my father.

I tried to come nearer to him after his passing, by finding out as much as I could about him and the context he grew up in. At first it was a process of trying to salvage whatever I had lost in the relationship. But in peeling back the layers, seeing the scabs from the scars which I thought had long healed, I was confronted instead with the far-reaching effects of trauma and of loss that went beyond just my relationship with him.

A few years after he died, I realised that I was still caught up in

PROLOGUE

a process of grieving that was in many ways all about the traumas of my childhood years. But now, I realised, while I was trying to regain something lost in the past, I was losing something in the present. While I was trying to restore something from the old world, I was tearing down the new world. While I was trying to heal old scars, I was inflicting fresh ones.

When my son Imani was five years old, his school set him a show-and-tell assignment about mammals. I thought that going to the Johannesburg Zoo as a family and taking pictures of him with different mammals in the background would make for a very cool presentation. At the zoo, Imani smiled and posed for each picture.

After spending almost the whole day at the zoo, we walked past the elephants' enclosure. They were big and majestic. There was a school party there. We joined in as the guide explained all the interesting facts about elephants to the learners. He spoke about their hooves and how soft and cushiony they are. 'They are like shock absorbers,' the guide expounded. 'While their feet look flat, they're actually walking on tiptoe. The area underneath what would be the heel of the foot is a soft, cartilage pad. This pad helps them to move silently. So as big as they are, they can actually pass next to your house as a herd without you hearing a thing.'

My son and I looked at each other with amazement. I would have thought they were the loudest mammals, especially in a herd. But elephants hardly make a sound when they are walking, we found out. On our way back home, my son turned to me. 'Daddy, I think only God can hear elephants walk,' he said. I just laughed.

But the truth is, there were few such light-hearted and uninhibited moments between us. Our relationship, in his early years, was characterised by me dressing him down, shouting at him, correcting him and generally breaking down his spirit at almost every turn. On some occasions I would even use my open hand to keep him in check.

Writing my memoir has been a way for me to revisit past traumas, to make sense of my narrative, often painfully. I hope it is also a way of shaping a future where those moments of closeness – when my children and I turn to each other in excitement and wonder – become our everyday.

PART 1

I

Mirror

A FATHER IS BORN

An image, my image
A disfigured sculpture of a strange man is my reflection
My eyes, vengeful and dead, stare and invite repulsion
An image so cold and empty, it turns roses to weeds
A lonely and sad man is what my reflection reads
An image, my image
I spend my days hurt and morose
Another man's faults are what my reflection poses
But I am a man, a man hidden in another man's form
I shower under a cold and violent storm
An image, my image
I fear not what I am, but I fear what I resemble
I fear looking upon myself decay and crumble
I have become what I most hate
An inevitable force, which my outcome dictates
An image, my image
My individuality is caught up in lies and pretence
I seek freedom of self but I'm a slave of inheritance
An image, my image

I was an angry teenager when I wrote these words in my scrapbook. It's a gloomy passage, assessing an uneasy and precarious relationship between a father and a son. The poem was one of two things I ever really wrote about my father, his obituary being the other, and each time I read the words I shudder at the desperation. I go over the lines with discomfort as I attempt to reconcile the 'strange man' with the one so many people spoke about so graciously on the day of his memorial service.

There's a part of me that wants to dismiss the writing as merely the ranting of a rebellious ingrate going through puberty, but there's another part of me that wants to embrace it as a true testimony to the sad nature of our relationship at the time. It's a conflict I've been mulling over ever since his passing on 3 March

2010, when he succumbed to diabetes, just a few weeks shy of his 55th birthday.

I don't know how much physical or emotional pain he was under, but I'd like to believe that he found a good death. When he took his last breath he was at home alone, huddled up in bed, and he was still wearing his pyjamas. By his bedside were two pocket-sized New Testament Bibles which included the books of Psalms and Proverbs. In the sky blue Setswana version of the Bible the book of Luke was marked at the end of Chapter 11 and at the beginning of Chapter 12. The navy blue English version of the Bible was marked at the book of Psalms, Chapters 33 and 34.

My father is the only one who can tell what verses he found reassuring in those final hours. But I wonder if he'd turned to the Word of God to ask of him some hard questions about life, his life. Could a footballing dream scuppered in its infancy because of a knee injury have been at the centre of his engagement with the Almighty? Or was he still agonising over his bitter divorce from my mother some seven years before, that had effectively ended their 25 years of marriage? Did he regret his harsh treatment of me and my big brother Tshepo, during our childhoods? I don't know. I can only wonder.

The first time I became aware of his diabetic condition was back in 2001, when I was doing my first year of study in journalism at the Technikon Pretoria, now called the Tshwane University of Technology. I had come home for the holidays and everything was still the same, at least on the exterior. Take my bedroom, for example. The iconic poster of hip-hop stars the Notorious B.I.G. and Puff Daddy gracing the red carpet at the 1997 Soul Train Awards was still affixed to the back of my bedroom door, and the two single beds with the matching vintage-styled headboards upholstered in brown polyester still occupied the far corners of the room. The only thing separating the two beds was my father's old Pioneer stereo system cabinet, with a glass door and trolley wheels, which I now used as a magazine rack.

My father was his usual distant self, present but absent, too occupied in his own thoughts to really engage with the rest of us. My mother Daisy was still energetic, trying out her hand at some new business, and my little brother Tumelo was his usual quiet-natured self, pleasant and still obsessed with Spider-Man. It was reassuring and constant.

But something had changed: my father's health. I picked it up one night when I was suddenly awoken by sounds of feet shuffling to the bathroom next to my bedroom. I heard a torrent of water being passed. It was my father. I thought nothing of it, and I went back to sleep. But hardly ten minutes passed before I was awoken again by the shuffling of feet and the passing of water. Thinking the whole thing comical and wondering if he had had too much water to drink, I let a snigger escape me. And then a little while later, as I was about to fall asleep again, the same thing happened. Now I was intrigued, not by the act itself, but by the abruptness and the frequency of it all. It would go on like that for the greater part of the night and the early morning too. I knew then that all was not well with him.

A medical report by a Dr Mphumelelo Gumbi, a general practitioner operating in Thokoza, states that my father first consulted with him in October 1997. Dr Gumbi diagnosed him with diabetes.

In March 2005 my father began to see a Dr Joshi Mukhesh, a specialist physician who diagnosed him with Type 2 diabetes. He was put on chronic medication: a combination of regular insulin injections to act as a substitute for his body's insulin and tablets to help lower his blood sugar levels. My research on the subject of diabetes after his passing led me to nocturia or nocturnal urination, a disorder where one suffers from a frequent need to get up in the night to pass water, affecting mostly older men and sometimes older women too. I found that the most relevant cause of this condition is uncontrolled diabetes, where more sugar appears in the urine, stimulating extra production of urine. This information helped me to put to bed finally the intrigue that had been lingering quietly at the back of my mind ever since the night of the shuffling of feet and the passing of water episode.

As a child I knew to never enquire after a grown-up's health. It was considered rude and a subject not up for discussion. So I never so much as attempted to ask of him, casually or respectfully, how he was doing. But I remember a cordial and a candid conversation we once had about his condition. I was 24 years old at the time and I was no longer living at home. I remember it because it happened so effortlessly, this cordial and candid conversation. He was driving me back to my place. All I knew of his sickness at the time was *o ne a tshweri ke tswekiri* – he had the sickness of the sugar. I thought that people with such a condition should always steer clear of eating sweet things. So I was surprised when I saw sweets sprawled in the centre console of his car.

'Should you be eating those?' I began, puzzled.

'What do you mean?' he asked.

'I mean with your sugar,' I said.

'It's actually called diabetes,' he corrected, and then he chuckled. 'Yes, I can eat sweets.' He explained that they were useful on some occasions, like when he'd been tied up in meetings the whole day and had not had anything to eat. 'They help with the dizzy spells that come with an empty stomach. But in general I try to stay away from sweet things as much as possible.'

'So how do you take your tea?' I asked.

He told me he took sweeteners.

'What about cool drinks?'

'I drink Tab cola because it's sugar free. I have Type 2 diabetes so I must constantly watch my blood sugar levels. The levels shouldn't be too high or too low.'

Thinking Type 2 diabetes was the severest form of diabetes I asked what he was doing about it to get it down to Type 1 at least.

'Type 1 is Type 1 and Type 2 is Type 2,' he said. 'One cannot go from Type 1 to Type 2 or vice versa. They are basically different forms of the same sickness. Some people are born with it, while others develop it over time.'

But I still wanted to know what he was doing about it.

'I'm on chronic medication,' he said.

Concerned, I asked how long he had to take it for.

'Chronic means I have to take the medication for life. There is no cure for diabetes. I can only manage it.' he said, rather upbeat.

I just nodded after that, pleasantly surprised by the frankness of our conversation. At the same time, I was saddened that his health had come to this. Here was a man who epitomised a healthy lifestyle. He had never drunk alcohol or smoked cigarettes in his life. He used to jog, and he remained fairly active with his soccer. But now he was a sickly man who constantly had to watch his sugar.

On 23 September 2005 my father saw Dr Mukhesh for the last time. I don't know why he decided to stop seeing him, but in the subsequent years he grew visibly frail. He was constantly fatigued. The lines around the corners of his eyes carved more definably when he smiled. His complexion turned dull and the skin around his cheeks hung loosely. His neck grew thin, and his Adam's apple became more prominent. The last remaining hairs on his balding crown disappeared rapidly. His posture started to cave in, and his demeanour turned sorrowful. This was all a far cry from the confident and upright stance that he had always had.

To make matters worse, his divorce from my mother was also finalised around that time. I felt sorry for him. But strangely enough our relationship progressed from being strained to being accommodating. I don't know if he was becoming less and less of the 'strange man' that I refer to in my poem or if I was becoming more and more accepting of him. But I still welcomed the progression nonetheless. I guess it was the cooling-off phase in what had otherwise been a tumultuous father-and-son relationship.

―――

This 'strange man' that I speak of in my poem first appeared to me when I was around five or six. Up until then my father had been a hero to me. I could sit on his lap, put my head against his chest and suck my thumb to sleep. I could tell my long tales to him, all day long, without him ever growing tired. He used to prop me up on his shoulders whenever he went to the shops, so I could enjoy a giant's view while feasting on some Simba chips and Creme Soda.

But this changed. He became someone I feared, with every ounce of my being. I feared the look in his eyes whenever he was upset about something. It was unflinching and penetrating. I feared the sound of his voice when he would berate us children. I would wet my short pants every time I heard it. I feared the smacks across the face and on the body which came lightning-fast and with a fury so fierce it was as if he were going up against someone his own size. The smacks would leave me dazed, puffy-eyed from crying, my ears buzzing, my face red hot, the back and the sides of my body branded with reddened five-finger print marks.

But I'd say my brother Tshepo, as the older one, had it worse. I remember an incident where he was pleading with my father,

A FATHER IS BORN

'*Wam'polaya! Wam'polaya!* You're killing me! You're killing me!' while he was being beaten against the walls and the wardrobe doors of our room.

Our relationship with our father was never warm or loving. We feared him and we only spoke to him when we were spoken to, really. This, at least in my case, progressed well into my young adult years. The scars never healed.

The last time I saw him alive was on 22 November 2009, just a couple of weeks after my wife Elrees had given birth to our son Imani. She had just undergone a kidney stone operation, during which she lost a lot of blood. The doctors had to perform a blood transfusion. After the transfusion I sent my mother and father a text message telling them the operation had been a success. My father sent a text message praising God for his good works.

The following day he, my mother and my younger brother Tumelo came to pay us a visit in hospital. My in-laws were also there. The mood in the visiting ward was cheerful. We were all very thankful to God that the kidney stone was finally out. I was playing about with my son. At some point I changed his nappy, and I gave him to his mother to be breastfed.

Observing all of this, my father simply said to me, 'I'm so proud of you, son.'

Everyone in the room was stunned, because my father had never been the kind of person to show affection. But it was sincere, and I was deeply moved. It was the kind of affirmation I had been longing for from him all these years. I think he was genuinely taken aback by how I had taken to being a father and a family man in such a short space of time. He was indeed truly proud.

———

On the morning of 2 March 2010 my father chaired what would later turn out to be his last staff meeting as the principal of Sechaba Primary School. My mother's older sister, Aunty Dolly, who was also a teacher at the school, told me that during the meeting my father kept complaining of a dry throat and asking for water. She said it did not matter how much water he drank, his thirst was just not quenchable. He left work early that day.

The following morning his condition had still not changed. At the time Tumelo was the only one living with him, because after the divorce my folks had decided that it was best for him to stay with my father. Their morning routine entailed my father dropping him off at school before he drove to work. But that morning he told Tumelo to walk to school because he wasn't feeling well. When he came home in the afternoon, at around 14:30, Tumelo found my father lying on his bed. He was not showing any signs of life. Tumelo tried to wake him up but he got no response, and so he called my mother and the emergency services. My mother rushed to the house, arriving just before the ambulance. The two paramedics took exactly ten minutes to assess the situation. Their report states that he was already dead upon their arrival.

———

When I got the call from my mother informing me of my father's sudden death, I was riding in a rackety taxi after work en route to a mechanic's place to pick up my wife's car. The taxi I was riding in was so noisy that I could hardly make out what she was saying. *Papa o thlokafetsi* – Your father has passed on,' she kept on saying, her voice rising with frustration each time. When I finally understood what she was saying I was stunned. I did not feel anything but surprise. I did not cry, nor was I sad. I was just stunned.

'OK, I'm on my way,' I said.

It was early evening when my wife and I arrived at my father's house. My father's younger sister M'shala and her daughter Mmapule were already busy clearing out the place to make room for the people who would come to offer their condolences. This hurt me. His place was my last piece of home, especially after the divorce. I wanted things to remain as they had been, at least for a little longer. I wanted to hang on to whatever memory was left of him, be it in the framed family photographs that he had hung across the walls, the vinyl records covered in dust, the wind chimes, the table ornaments, the clocks, big and small, that he had kept in almost every room of the house or the outdated encyclopaedias that still occupied the bookshelf in the lounge. I felt as if his body was not even cold but his memory was already being wiped out.

I threw a tantrum, and they stopped clearing out the place. Then suddenly I felt a flood of emotion rising up, the kind of emotion that brings you up against your own mortality, the kind that lies dormant for years and then comes gushing up for air, for all to see.

Nothing had prepared me for this moment. I couldn't help but feel cheated by his death. I felt that he had been taken away too soon. I felt that we had been making good progress with our relationship over the last couple of years and now it was all for nothing. He was gone, and I didn't even get a chance to say goodbye. Before I knew it, I broke down. I cried bitterly, in front of everyone. I cried and I cried. My mother's younger sister *Mmangwane* Manana tried to comfort me by reminding me that at least he got to see me pay *magadi* for my wife – following the traditional Pedi arrangement, where the groom's family gives money to the bride's family – and that he also got the chance to see me become a father, so he was at peace. But I was still inconsolable.

―

Some months later I asked myself why I was so gutted by his passing, why I was so emotional about someone who I felt had tormented me, why I was so shattered by the loss of someone who had physically and psychologically abused me, someone whose open-hand and backhand smacks across the face and on my body as a child made me wet myself. Why I cried my eyes out so bitterly for this 'strange man' whose image was 'cold and empty' and whose dominance over my life had enslaved my freedom of self.

And then it hit me that in spite of our imperfect relationship I actually did love this man. It is a difficult thing to admit but I truly did love him. My father was always present in my life. I cannot ever imagine a time when he was not around. He was always there. This is the man who built me up but also a man who broke me down, a man who left me scarred but also a man who made me strong. I decided to forgive him for his strict and heavy-handed child-rearing style. He was a product of his time, I reasoned. A sense of nostalgia and love came over me.

But one day, while looking in the proverbial mirror of self-reflection, I saw a distance between me and my son Imani. A distance frighteningly similar to the one that had lain between my father and me. I saw the gap between us widening with each passing day. I saw him reaching out to me, and me struggling to relate to him. I saw myself panel-beating him into this person that I thought he should be, instead of just embracing the person that he was.

I saw myself hopelessly struggling to discern between discipline and punishment, falling back instinctively on what my father had taught me. I saw how I was affecting Imani's confidence with my cold silent treatments when he had been naughty. At its worst, I saw myself lashing out in anger at him and I saw him pinching his member in fear, afraid that he might wet himself.

I was embarrassed and I was saddened. They say a mirror never lies. If that's the truth, then my reflection was of a broken man. *What good is a present father if he doesn't know how to love*, I asked myself. Do I even know what love is? I wanted to break this mirror, to shatter it into a million pieces so I could see no more of this reflection, of this truth staring back at me.

Then something inside of me told me to rather change the image instead. But I knew that in order to do that, I first needed to understand who I was. I needed to understand the difficult events of my childhood, the sometimes incomprehensible choices I had made as I struggled towards manhood, marriage and fatherhood.

I decided to start by trying to truly understand who my father had been, and the forces that had shaped him.

2

'*O mang? Wa ga mang?*'
'Who are you? Whose child are you?'

O mang?
Tumiso.
Wa ga mang?
Mashaba.
Oh, so you are Shangaan?
No, Pedi.
But there's no such thing as a Mashaba who is Pedi. The Mashabas are Shangaan!

This is the kind of interaction I usually encounter from strangers with a supposedly 'superior' knowledge of my roots. It does not matter how truthfully I answer these questions, my responses are always unsatisfactory and you'd think that I'd just committed the worst crime imaginable when my questioners learn that I can't even *vula vula* – speak Xitsonga – to save my life. As a child I used to feel that these questions, seemingly well meaning on the surface and mostly from grown-ups, were really designed to catch me out in a lie. They also used to make me feel like I was denying my own culture, like I was running away from my heritage.

I remember coming home once as a child after one such grilling from a grown-up. I was riled up and close to tears. When my father asked me why I was so upset I told him that people out there were calling us Shangaans. He just looked at me and chuckled, and he told me to not take it to heart. He assured me that we really were Pedi. I was comforted, because in those days Shangaan people in the townships were – I guess they still are – to some extent looked down upon. When I was growing up, the stereotypes about them were many and unflattering. Their language was considered gibberish and only good enough to be made fun of. Their style of dress was deemed unnecessarily loud and flamboyant. Their complexion was judged to be too dark to be beautiful. Their men were thought to be nothing more than oily mechanics who fixed cars and their women were dismissed as baby-making machines with no concept of family planning. The worst was the story of how, when Shaka Zulu and his men were advancing against them during the Mfecane period, they were so filled with fear that they literally ran and left their children behind. They were then labelled *'Ama-shiya-ngane,'* an isiZulu phrase which simply means the ones who abandoned their children, hence the name Shangaan.[1]

As a grown-up I've come to appreciate South Africa's rich and diverse cultural heritage, and I'm also of the view now that being a Mushangaan is really of no consequence – no more than being a Motswana, Muvenda or Indebele, for example, is.

While my father was alive he never shared with me any information about our family, such as who we are and where we come from, or *direto* – the oral literature that contains one's family history and totems that is passed down through praise-singing. He was not a man who was deeply rooted in culture and tradition. Either he saw himself as a modernised man who didn't have to bother much with matters of culture and tradition, or he too simply didn't know much about his heritage. So when he passed, I decided to take it upon myself to find out the true origins of the Mashabas, not only to have a better understanding of my roots but to also preserve that knowledge somehow for future generations.

---

1 This story is not true because, according to the Nhlapo Commission on Traditional Leadership Disputes and Claims, which was set up in 2004 by the former president, Thabo Mbeki, the name Shangaan or amaShangana actually comes from Soshangana, a military commander of the amaNdwandwe. After the defeat of the amaNdwandwe by Shaka in 1819, Soshangana refused to be incorporated into the Zulu kingdom. He fled instead with his followers along the eastern foothills of the Lubombo mountains to the upper Tembe River. Soshangana and his followers later crossed the Tembe River to Delagoa Bay. There he fought, defeated and subjugated the Thonga communities he found in the area. He then moved further north to an area known as Bileni. On his way to Bileni, Soshangana subjugated and incorporated indigenous communities that included the Ndzawu, the Ngomane, the Shongonono, the Rhonga, the Chopi, the Shona and the Tshwa. Thus, Soshangana established his kingdom. The report is available at: https://static.pmg.org.za/docs/100729determination-chiefs.pdf (Acccessed 1 July 2021).

The first thing I learnt about the surname is that it comes from the Ndau clan, who inhabit the Zambezi valley in central Mozambique and also the eastern part of Zimbabwe, south of Chipinge and Chimanimani. The second thing I learnt is that Mashaba is a Tsonga surname and not Shangaan, with the variants Maxava, Machava and Machaba. I make the distinction between Tsonga and Shangaan because while they do share a common language, culture and even blood, there are some people who feel they do not necessarily share a common political history and should therefore not be clustered or defined as one homogeneous group under the Shangaan banner.

If the Mashabas are Tsonga, are the Mashabas who consider themselves Pedi, like me, Pedi by alliance, assimilation or conquest? When, after my father died, I contacted *Rremogolo* Frank, the son of my grandfather's older brother Mashatole, he told me that none of the assertions are correct, because Mashaba is actually a 'borrowed' surname. He said that we are in fact *Banareng baga Mohlala,* which means we are the people of Mohlala who belong to the greater Banareng clan, and the Buffalo (*Nare* in Sepedi) is our family totem. He explained the 'borrowed' surname part thus:

> A long time ago, one of our ancestors, a Mohlala, had many wives. He was a wealthy man. He had everything a man could ask for in those days except for children. For a long time, the man and his many wives kept trying to have children, but to no avail. Then one day a traditional healer from Mozambique settled in his village. News soon spread of the traditional healer's amazing works. With nothing to lose, the man decided to pay this traditional healer a visit. The traditional healer gave him some herbs to try out. He went back home and after some time his youngest wife gave birth to a son, a true *mojalefa* – an heir. Overjoyed, the man went back to the traditional healer to thank

him. When he got there, he told him that there was no money or treasure in the world that could properly express his gratitude. As a show of his everlasting appreciation, he told the traditional healer that he would name his son after him. The traditional healer's name was Mashaba, and that's how we all came to be Mashaba.

I tried hard not to laugh in *Rremogolo* Frank's presence, but I didn't know which story I found more preposterous, the *'Amashiya-ngane'* story or this one. But *Rremogolo* attested to it. He did, however, manage to give me something more substantive, our family tree. It's a family tree that goes back four generations, beginning with my great-great-grandfather Dinomoko:

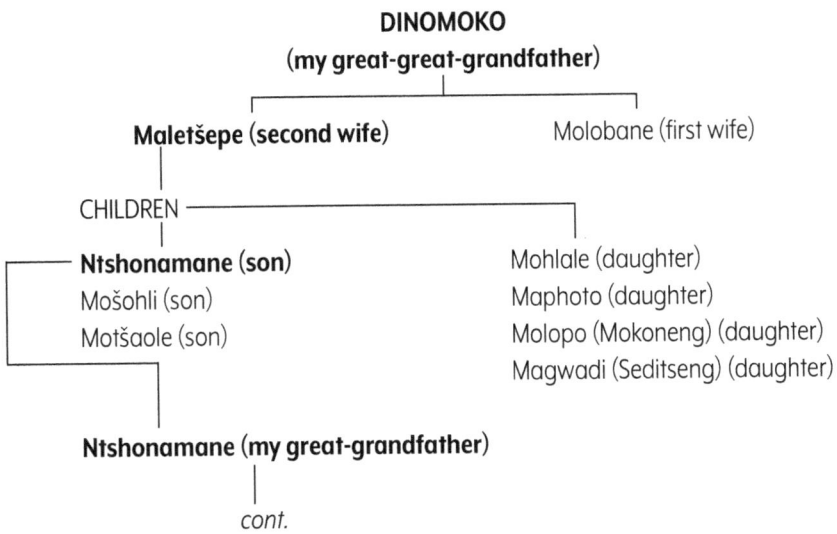

A FATHER IS BORN

Ntshonamane (my great-grandfather)

Modipi (wife) — Maleaki (wife)

CHILDREN

Sello (son)
Dikelepe (son)
Mashatole (son) ———————— CHILDREN = Frank (son); Irene (daughter)
Hlamphane (son)   and the others
Tshungwane (son) (my grandfather) ———— **Wife = Kgaša (my grandmother)**
Morakeng (son)
Morudi (daughter)
Nthosana (daughter)

CHILDREN

Madikgonane/Boy (son)
Maletšepe (Matsatsi) (daughter)
Dinomoko Neo (son) (my father)
Moshala (daughter)
Twins ———— Madimabe (Mbuti) (son)
             Maniki (daughter)
Thabo (son)

Dinomoko Neo (my father) ———— **Dikeledi Daisy (wife) (my mother)**

CHILDREN

Tshepo (son) (late)
Tumiso (son) me ———————— **Wife = Elrees**
Tumelo (son)

CHILDREN

Synové (daughter) (late)
Imani (son)
Neo (daughter)

What I find most fascinating about this family tree are the subtle but poignant linkages between the past and the present. When my father was born, he was named Dinomoko by my grandfather, after my great-great-grandfather. He is the only one in the family ever to have been named after him. My father's big sister Maletšepe, on the other hand, got her name from my great-great-grandfather's second wife. When my daughter was born, I named her Neo after my father as a way of keeping his memory alive, and also because Neo was the name he much preferred over the historically heavy Dinomoko. His English name was Whitey. I'm told my grandmother named him so because he was such a fair-skinned baby. But what if my father had come out a dark-skinned baby? Would my grandmother have named him Darkie? I can only imagine.[2]

When I said goodbye to *Rremogolo* Frank, I thanked him for passing down such valuable information about my family. But despite this new knowledge I still found myself a man none the wiser when it came to the true origins of the Mashabas. *Maybe we really are of Ndau origin*, I thought to myself. Surnames and family totems could have been shared or exchanged during the interactions and the cross-marriages between the Ndau people and various other clans, much like the Sitholes who can be found amongst the Zulus, the Ndebeles and also the Swatis, I reasoned.

But I was still not entirely satisfied. I decided to do some more research. I stumbled upon an online piece written by historian Dr

---

2   That choice of a name seems quite quirky and light-hearted, but I also believe that names have the propensity to determine what type of a person an individual turns out to be. When *Rrangwane* Mbuti, my father's younger brother, was born, he was named Madimabe, which literally means 'bad blood'. He was so named because he was a very sickly baby, and in Sepedi culture it is believed that naming a baby in the negative actually helps it grow strong and healthy. Indeed, he grew to be strong and healthy, but the negative sentiment attached to the name remained with him throughout his life. For example, his wife Grace left him after only a couple of years of marriage because of his heavy drinking. To this day he has not remarried and he still drinks heavily.

A FATHER IS BORN

Mpho Mohlala on the history of the Mohlalas. About a year after my father died, I sent Dr Mohlala an email enquiring about the history of the Mashaba people and how they fit into the greater Banareng community. About five months later he responded, with a greeting '*Monareng/Motlokwa!*' followed by an apology for taking such a long time to get back to me.

'Others indicate that Mashaba comes from Mozambique (Shangaan) hence *Mashaba-a-Mashashamela* (Xaixai in Mozambique),' he explained. However, he said, he didn't buy that. 'The Tsonga Mashabas are from Mozambique, but the *Banareng ba Mashaba* are the children of Seege, hence we have *Mashaba-a-Seege*. This means Seege's people, community or folk. '*Ka Sepedi re nale Leshaba la batho and Mashaba a batho*' – which translates to the nation of Mashaba. Seege, by the way, was either one of the children or a grandchild of Mohlala-Morudi.'

When I delved deeper into the history of the Banareng as recorded by the Mohlalas, I found that it's a long history characterised by the clan's constant changes in identity. These date from the 1500s when the father and the founder of the clan, Kgoši Mphele (*Mphela'a ngwato*), and his son Zulu first settled in Botswana after trekking all the way down from the Great Lakes region in Central Africa. For example, when a splinter group of the Banareng led by one Mokgopedi (the son of Mohlala Sebushi) got to Botlokwa in Limpopo in the 1600s they were conquered by the Bakgalaka (the children of Tlokwe) and there they became Batlokwa. When another splinter group arose out of the Banareng and the Batlokwa alliance they were again conquered by the Bakgatla while they were on their way to Chuniespoort. There they became *Bakone ba Matlala*, and the *Banareng ba Mashaba*, as it turns out, are but a grouping amongst other groupings like the Paledis, the Ranthos, the Molekes, the Mashas and so on – groups that were all either conquered or adopted by the greater *Banareng ba Mohlala* clan.

When I was born my father named me Kingdom. I don't know why he gave me such an unusual, biblical name. It's not like Peter, John or Samuel. It's rather abstract in its nature: an idea, a vision, a kind of utopian ever-after that may or may not exist.

It's a name that I carried with no particular care until my first day of school. I was excited to be in big school finally. I did not have any of the anxieties usually associated with first-time schoolgoers, such as crying for mommy, for example. I was just in my element. My white, short-sleeved shirt was bright and crisp, my black shorts were spotless, my grey socks were pulled up to my knees and my Toughees school shoes were snug and immaculate. I think everything I had on that day was new, including my underwear. Our classroom teacher was a Miss Mokoena, a slender woman in her early thirties who kept a small, neat Afro and wore smart blouses and plaid wool skirts that went over her knees.

Her first instruction of the day was for each child to come up to the front of the class and introduce themselves. One by one the kids went up, said their names and then took their seats again. When it was my turn I walked up to the front of the class with a confident stride and with my chest puffed out, just as my big brother Tshepo had coached me to do. I introduced myself clearly and affirmatively.

'My name is Kingdom Mashaba!' I said.

But my spirited introduction was met with some chortling from the class.

Chortling? But why?

Miss Mokoena promptly hushed everyone up. Unsure of what had just happened, I went back to take my seat, a little less confident now. When it was break time some kids from my class kept following me around and taunting me about my name. I tried to shake them off, but they just wouldn't let up. When the second

A FATHER IS BORN

break came they did the same thing, following me around and teasing me about my name.

I can't remember what the exact taunt was. Maybe it was in the way they said the name. I don't remember. But it was just awful. When I got home that day I told my father that I didn't want to be called Kingdom any more. He looked at me, smiled, and he said, 'OK, you don't have to use that name any more.'

By the following week I was just Tumiso, not Kingdom, just Tumiso. My father was a teacher at the school and that's why I think my 'name-situation' was resolved so speedily. Miss Mokoena made sure that all the kids called me Tumiso, and she told them that if they called me anything else then there would be serious trouble. So the name was wiped out from all of my school records. The only place where you could still find the name was on my father's Bonitas medical aid card, under the list of dependants. But in essence Kingdom was gone. Kingdom was dead. Of course, there were some kids here and there, mostly girls, who still tried their luck with the name. Luckily I was the kind of kid who knew how to throw a punch to the stomach, and not just any punch but the kind of punch that sucked all the air out of the stomach.

When I think about this incident I'm surprised by how cool my father was about the whole thing. I wonder how things would've turned out if my father, as a youngster, had walked up to my paternal grandfather, who was Tshungwane, and told him that he didn't want to be called by his name, Dinomoko, any more. I don't think it's a movie that ends well at all. I don't see my grandfather acceding to his wishes to change his name. Instead, I see my grandfather pulling out his belt and whipping some sense into him.

I believe names, whether given or inherited, are important for any individual because they serve as an important identity feature and also as an important link between the individual and his or her ancestors. But I think there was a clear design to my father's 'madness' when he acceded to me dropping the name Kingdom. I think he understood the importance of having the freedom to define oneself, because contrary to popular belief, one's identity is actually not absolute. In fact, as in the case of my clan's constantly changing identity, it is rather fluid. My father wasn't sentimental at all about the name he had given me, even though he himself couldn't change or drop his inherited name Dinomoko.

I think the freedom to define myself was one of the best gifts that he ever gave to me. It was an invaluable gift that simply allowed me to be. It was a gift of identity and at the same time it was a gift of being free to redefine that very identity.

3

First born third

My father, Dinomoko Neo Whitey, was born on 24 March 1955 in a township called Payneville, a place that came into being between 1930 and 1940 on the East Rand of Johannesburg near Springs. Payneville was created as a direct result of a booming coal and gold mining industry, for the benefit of black, Indian and coloured labourers who came to work in the mines and other industries of the small town.

My paternal grandfather, Tshungwane, was a mineworker at the time while my grandmother, his wife Kgaša, worked in the kitchens as a maid and as a childminder. They were both from Lydenburg or Mashishing, close to Pilgrim's Rest, in what is now Mpumalanga, and they were also something like kissing cousins. I have no evidence to verify that the two were really related, but the practice of marrying a second, a third, a fourth or even a fifth cousin was quite common in those days.

My grandmother was the fifth out of six children born to Tshakgate and Mojakgomo. She was born on 1 January 1929. I remember her as a kind-hearted and soft-spoken woman with an easy laugh. She was fair-skinned, had full cheeks, a strong jawline and a smile full of teeth. She was of medium build. She had strong legs and she seemed to never tire of hard work. Rarely would anyone hear *Ousi* Pina, as she was affectionately known, complain about anything.

My grandfather, on the other hand, was quite a crass fellow, a straight-talker who cared little about other people's feelings. He was born on 24 April 1912. He was the fifth-born child in a family of eight children, comprising six sons and two daughters of Ntshonamane and his second wife Modipi. He was a dark-skinned man with a permanent Popeye the Sailor Man air of smugness about him. He had a bony, skeletal frame and, judging by the only picture that I have of him from the 1960s, which shows him standing in his backyard with his hands on his hips, indifferent in his demeanour. I'd say his clothes actually wore the man.

A FATHER IS BORN

Rrangwane Mbuti remembers him as a very stubborn, short-tempered and foul-mouthed man. 'He used to insist on riding his bicycle to work every day because he felt the bus fare was just way too expensive,' he recalls. 'Come rain or shine, he would ride his bicycle. Then one day, and ironically so, he got hit by a bus while riding to work. Luckily, he came out unscathed, but the bicycle was not so lucky. Instead of throwing the mangled thing away he brought it back with him in hopes of fixing it. I felt it was just cluttering an already small yard of the house and so I threw it away. When he found out he was not impressed at all. He hurled all sorts of expletives at me – *'Jou moerskont'* (Your mother's private parts) being at the top of that list. To appease him I promised to buy his weekly bus coupons out of my own pocket. The cheapskate agreed,' he told me.

My grandfather probably came to Springs in the mid 1930s as a twenty-something young man seeking some kind of fortune. Or maybe he had been sent from home to seek after his older brothers who hadn't been home in years now. Either way, when he arrived, probably by bus and possibly with a worn-out briefcase that held his only possessions, he must've felt that staying and making a living for himself in Springs was much better than going back to the doldrums of Mashishing.

Maybe he stayed with one of his brothers for a good while as a squatter, and that same brother was the one who organised him a job at one of the surrounding mines. After working for some time, he probably saved up enough money to move out of his brother's place and get himself a single room at the male hostels. There, his life would have revolved around drinking alcohol excessively, mixing and mingling with different women and going to work.

I venture so because Tshungwane only got to father his first child, Madikgonane, or Boy as he was commonly known, in 1948 when he was in his mid-thirties. This was considered late for someone to start a family in those days. His family back home in Mashishing probably felt that it was unbecoming of a young man (who was fast becoming an old man) to be leading such an aimless lifestyle, and so they probably took it upon themselves to send my grandmother Pina to look after him, to bring some stability in his life and to help him 'build a home' as it were. Or maybe he was just sick and tired of being single and so he pounced upon the 18-year-old Pina, who had probably just arrived in Springs fresh off the bus, and being the innocent, country bumpkin girl that she was, couldn't help but fall for the old man's schemes. Whatever the scenario, some semblance of structure did take shape when my grandmother came into his life.

Boy was born in 1948. In 1951, about two years later, my grandparents welcomed their second-born and first girl child in the family in Mmatsatsi. About two months after my father was born, on 19 June 1955, he was baptised at the Evangelical Lutheran Church in Payneville. My grandfather was never much of a churchgoer but my grandmother was a devout Lutheran, a true *mme wa seaparo* – a woman who dons the black and white uniform of the church every Sunday without fail – and that's why I suspect that it was her decision really to have my father baptised as an infant.

While my grandmother was religious in a traditional way, my grandfather might have been said to have a religious relationship with skokiaan, the home brew made by township brewers. He is almost certain to have witnessed some of the protests against police raids on domestic brewers. A *Rand Daily Mail* report of 14 August 1938 describes a hundred armed men descending on Payneville at four o'clock in the morning, arresting 70 women and 360 men and confiscating a thousand gallons of illicit beer.

Records from the Native Affairs Department and the Springs Police from 16 to 18 September 1940 paint a harrowing picture of how miners and brewers hit back:

A FATHER IS BORN

On the 15th of September 1940 the police were called into Payneville to stop a fight between a hundred Basotho and Xhosa miners. But as soon as they arrived the erstwhile combatants united and the police found themselves the target of the attack. Women shouted 'attack the police' and a general offensive was launched against them. So fierce was the onslaught that the police felt compelled to shoot their way out, leaving two of the crowd dead and two wounded. Six white and one African police men were injured in the disturbance.

In Payneville, protests against raids of illicit brewers continued until the early 1950s. I wonder if my grandfather ever joined in these protests. But one thing I am certain of, he was definitely a regular customer of these domestic brewers.[3]

A 1930s survey of the Reef locations by the Non-European and Native Affairs Department[4] shows that by 1939 Payneville had 561 municipally built houses. The two- or sometimes three-bedroomed houses of the township were often called 'matchbox' houses because they were small, square structures that looked identical to one another. The houses were built from bricks and mortar and had corrugated iron or asbestos cement sheet roofing. But their ablution facilities were abysmal and the people living there used bucket toilets. The municipality also

---

3 Home-brewing of beer in the township had been a common practice from the day of the first arrivals there. But in 1938 the municipality of Springs began selling 'kaffir beer'. This peculiarity was actually in line with a 1937 amendment to the Natives (Urban Areas) Act which now compelled local authorities to either establish municipal monopolies over beer or to permit domestic brewing. In order for the 'kaffir beer' to find a market in Payneville, the authorities had to first clamp down on domestic brewing. This information comes from Philip Bonner's '"Desirable or undesirable Sotho women?" Liquor, prostitution and the migration of Sotho women to the Rand, 1920–1945'. Available at: https://core.ac.uk/download/pdf/39667365.pdf. (Accessed 19 June 2021).

4 Non-European and Native Affairs Department Survey of Reef Locations, May 1939. Available at: http://www.historicalpapers.wits.ac.za/inventories/inv_pdft/A2628/A2628-B1-text.pdf (accessed 19 June 2021).

built single rooms that were cemented together in four blocks of 12 rooms each, to cater for single males. The township also had 888 privately built houses. Because these houses were built from Kimberley (unbaked) bricks and were not subject to strict technical supervision during construction, the municipality began a process of eliminating them in the early 1940s.

The survey shows that Payneville had a large sports ground near the entrance of the township. It had two football grounds and a cycle track; 'native' and 'Eurafrican' tennis courts; a communal recreation hall where a weekly 'bioscope' was shown; and the municipal beer hall that had been built in 1938. Payneville had one government school for 'Eurafricans', three missionary-run schools which were state-aided, and several smaller private schools.

My mother Daisy, who used to visit the place as a little girl, remembers Payneville with fondness. She says when it was time to do laundry, people used to walk to a place called *Ko matlapeng*, a rocky place which was close to a stream. 'It was a sight akin to the Ganges in India,' she tells me. Another fond memory of hers is the road-and-rail bridge on the Welgedacht route between Springs and Payneville. The road-and-rail bridge, which is still in existence, is so steep that when a vehicle goes over the bridge, especially at high speed, it feels like a rollercoaster, especially when it is coming down. My mother says they used to scrounge for bus fare money to go to town, not for the shopping, but just for the rush they got whenever they rode over the bridge.

Between 1939 and 1951 there were no more new houses being built in Payneville. Minutes from the Springs Public Health and Non-European Committee meeting in 1957[5] indicate that

---

5   Nieftagodien, N. 'The making of apartheid in Springs during the sixties: Group areas, urban restructuring and resistance', 15 April 1996. Available at: https://core.ac.uk/download/pdf/39668252.pdf (accessed 19 June 2021).

by 1952, three years before my father was born, the population of Payneville was 33 000. According to the municipal council, this figure was alarmingly high for a township that was originally designed to cater for only 8 000 people. In response to the 'overcrowding' or lack of housing, the council set up an 'emergency camp' which would later become the Jabavu section of the township.

But on 2 December 1952 Jabavu would be struck down by a deadly tornado. The violent tornado swept through the township, claimed 11 lives and left a devastating trail of destruction in its wake. People's homes and possessions were in utter ruin. My mother's older brother Uncle Zakes, who was still a baby at the time, still bears a scar on his forehead from when a flying zinc roof sheet struck him on the head on that fateful day.

Fortunately, the first three streets of a new township for Africans, built near the Vlakfontein mining area, which was about 15 kilometres away from Springs, had been completed by then and so the victims of the tornado could be accommodated immediately. That's how Kwa-Thema, named after political activist Selope Thema, and the first section, Tornado, named after the natural disaster, first came into being. Kwa-Thema was sold as a modernist development offering 'more congenial living conditions' for black industrial workers by the National Building Research Institute after they had been approached by the Town Council of Springs in 1950 to assist them with planning a new and separate native township within their municipal area, and it was to become the blueprint for all the other subsequent townships in the East Rand.[6]

I don't know when exactly my grandparents moved to Kwa-Thema or the circumstances surrounding that move, but what

---

6 D.M. Calderwood. 'An approach to low cost urban native housing in South Africa'. *The Town Planning Review*, Vol. 24, No. 4 (January 1954).

I know for sure is that they, together with their three children, were living as backroom squatters or tenants in Payneville. When houses became available in Kwa-Thema, as a direct result of the systematic transfer of black people from Payneville by the apartheid government, I presume that they were more than happy to move. In Kwa-Thema they moved into a semi-detached four-roomed house on Nhlengetwa Street in Masimini section. The asbestos-roofed house with a rough cement coating on its walls had a small kitchen with a Welcome Dover coal stove and an outside toilet with a flushing pull chain on its high-level cistern. My grandfather never bothered to paint the house outside, nor to erect a fence. He grew a hedge around the house instead. It's only in recent times that a fence was built. He also planted a grape tree just by the gate to provide the perfect shade on sunny days.

It was here in Kwa-Thema that my father's path in life changed forever.

One day, when he was seven years old, his older brother Boy collapsed mysteriously while he was walking home from school. Hearing of the news from a passer-by, the family rushed to his aid with a wheelbarrow. But by the time they got there it was too late. Boy was gone.

He was only 13 years old at the time. No one knows what really happened to him. Some say it was something he ate at school and others say it was a severe case of dehydration, because of how he had complained of a nagging headache several days prior.

Boy's was the first death in the family that my father would experience, and it was also one that would greatly shape his upbringing. It catapulted him to *abuti* or big brother status. As the big brother, he would grow up being treated with respect and tip-toed around by his younger siblings, Mosalasuping (M'shala), the twins Mbuti and Maniki and the last-born, Thabo, and he was admonished only with kid gloves by his mother.

But not so by Tshungwane, who was always hard on him. My

My paternal grandparents, Tshungwane and Pina

father got hidings from my grandfather until he was well into his teens because he loved to play dice, a vice most detested by my grandfather. Whenever word got out that my father was gambling again in the streets then a serious straightening-out was sure to follow.

I think my father's original birth-order position in the Tshungwane household was quite an enviable one, because by the time he was born he had two older siblings, who were really the 'trial and error babies' for lack of a better phrase. I'd like to believe that, as the new baby in the family at the time, he was well looked after and doted upon by his older siblings, especially by Mmatsatsi, who would always have a soft spot for him. But all this changed.

My father shouldered the burden of excessive responsibility from a very early age. He had to assume firstborn duties, like being sent out on errands or being charged with the care of his younger siblings, and I believe that this played a big role in shaping his personality and emotional development. All of which shaped the kind of father he would become.

Even though there is no conclusive scientific evidence to show a direct relationship between birth order and personality, I believe that Boy's death changed the hierarchical make-up of the family and that it had an impact on my father's character. Had Boy lived beyond his teenage years, for example, I believe my father would have turned out a very different child and ultimately adult. The spotlight and attention would have been on Boy, as the firstborn and male child. My father, as the middle child, would have probably grown to be the 'overlooked' one, who stayed in his own shell, or at best the 'overindulged' carefree child who was completely free to be himself. Instead, he would grow to be a steadfast, disciplined, domineering figure who was quick to anger. An individual who would grow to shoulder most of the family's responsibilities.

4

A father is born

A FATHER IS BORN

My father's first love was undoubtedly soccer. I'm told that he was quite the soccer star in his day. But details of his heroics on the field of play are rather scant.

'Your father was an amazing footballer!' is the answer I always get whenever I ask about that part of his life. There are no scintillating anecdotes of a daring attacking midfielder who could easily whizz past defenders from the halfway line, rainbow-flick the ball over a dazed goalkeeper and then back-heel it past the goalposts. There are no old newspaper clippings whose reports have him as a saviour who comes off the bench in the second half of the game to rescue his team from a near defeat with a thundering strike from the offensive third of the pitch. Yet the legend of Professor Snow White continues to live on amongst his contemporaries.

But when I look at pictures from his football playing days as a young man, I'm tempted to surmise that he was indeed the amazing footballer that family and friends claim he was. For starters, he took great pride in the way he looked. In most of his pictures his soccer boots are tightly fastened, his socks are pulled up to his knees, his strip is clean and well-fitting and his hair is neatly combed out.

'If you look sloppy then your performance on the field of play or in life in general will also be sloppy, but if you look sharp then your performance will be as sharp as the way you look,' I remember he used to say.

I'd say he was also in great physical shape. He was of medium height. His frame was lean and ripped. His stature was proud and confident, and he walked *ka matsetsekwane* – with a tiptoed bounce to his step. There's a particular photo where he is bare chested, and he is rope-skipping outside at some school. The image shows perfectly how well chiselled his body was. Every contour from his shoulders to his calves is noticeably pronounced, particularly his abs. The poised look on his face tells of a footballer who took his training regimen seriously. But the knee-guard on his left knee is indicative of a recurring knee injury. In the background of the picture there's a boy carrying a soccer ball who is running towards him in awe, presumably to gain a better view of the skip-roping session that is captured in the frame.

In *The Rediscovery of the Ordinary: Essays on South African Literature and Culture*, Njabulo Ndebele writes that in those days 'spectacular display of individual talent [was] often more memorable, more enjoyable, and ultimately, even more desirable than the final score', and this enjoyment is certainly something I see

in my father's demeanour. There are pictures of him juggling and dribbling, and even a horribly staged 'selling of a dummy to a teammate' picture, that all point to a footballer who had a flair for the theatrics. What stands out for me is the peculiar way in which he carries his hands, limp-wristed and bent inward in a beak- or hook-like manner. I don't know why, but in the townships while I was growing up it was widely believed that if a footballer kept his hands in that way while playing, then he was exceptionally talented – the sort who could move with a swift, swan-like flair on the pitch. A footballer who best typified this was the legendary Kaizer Chiefs midfielder Doctor '16V' Khumalo.

My father's starting eleven pictures show him to have been a jolly fellow who enjoyed the camaraderie of his teammates. In these pictures his face is either beaming with quiet contentment or bursting with uncontainable joy, but he is never withdrawn from his teammates.

A footballer in those days was never really complete without a nickname or two, and my father had quite a couple. In *African Soccerscapes: How a Continent Changed the World's Game,* author and African history professor Peter Alegi says the culture of nicknames in football came from the tradition of praise singing and praise names from the homesteads. Alegi says a footballer's physical attributes or technical abilities often inspired their nicknames from the fans. My father's prowess earned him nicknames like 'Shakes', 'Maria Maria', 'Snowball' and the most popular, 'Professor Snow White'. 'Shakes' was obviously taken from the legendary Ephraim 'Shakes' Mashaba. 'Maria Maria' I'm told was inspired by his nimble-footedness or the dancing-feel that his playing style evoked. 'Snowball' was both a reference to his light-skinned complexion and to the damage a good and hardened snowball thrown at high speed could do. 'Professor Snow White' was simply a play on both Snowball and his English name Whitey.

My mother says my father was born at the wrong time, and

would have gone far with the right support to nurture his talent. She told me that he used to play for Tlakula High School alongside the likes of Nick 'Yster' Sikwane (former Kaizer Chiefs wing-back), while Nelson 'Teenage' Dladla (former Kaizer Chiefs midfielder) and Andries 'Six Mabone' Maseko (former Moroka Swallows striker) used to play for Phulong High School.

'When these two schools met for a match the whole of Kwa-Thema would literally come to a standstill,' she remembered. 'It was like a derby game. The rivalry between these two schools was so intense that no one wanted to miss out on the action.'

According to her, my father was a light-footed midfielder who played on tiptoe as if he were dancing. He was a dribbling wizard who could do anything with the ball. He could flick it over defenders with ease or he could keep it close to his feet like a magnet, making it almost impossible for anyone to get it from him.

My father's prowess certainly attracted my mother. While my father played for Tlakula High School she was a cheerleader for the rival Phulong School. 'Instead of cheering for our school, Phulong, we would cheer for Tlakula with all of our might. But in reality we were cheering for our boyfriends, your father and his friend Yster,' she told me, with the sparkle of a love-struck teenager in her eyes, when I interviewed her.

She said the second half of the game would always be delayed because they used to walk up to the halfway line of the pitch during half-time to cheer at the tops of their voices. 'The referee would have no choice but to wait for us to finish,' she said. 'But come Monday morning we'd be in so much trouble at school, especially if Tlakula had won the game. Our teacher Mr Sethushi would call us out during assembly, and he would brand us as traitors in front of everyone, and after that he'd give us a good whacking on our hands with a cane. But that still didn't stop us from cheering for our boyfriends come the next game,' she added with a wry smile.

A FATHER IS BORN

While I do appreciate her insights, I still do not understand exactly what my father did on the football field to warrant such praise and adoration.

My father's best friend, Themba Bukhale, said he first met my father when they were both just 15 years old. 'He was playing for a team called United Birds at the time and I was playing for Home Sweepers, and because he was such a good player I kept trying to recruit him into our team. But every time I would ask him he would just say, "*Ntwana,* you guys at Home Sweepers won't be able to keep up with me." I understood why he was so reluctant, because back then it wasn't easy for a soccer player to just switch teams. People used to get stabbed for doing that.'

Some years later the two of them met up again in Germiston at a football club called Katlehong City (formerly known as Germiston Callies). The team was fairly successful and they even had a stint playing in the second division of the National Premier Soccer League.

Themba Bukhale was the best man at my parents' wedding in 1978. 'At the wedding reception the priest kindly asked me as the best man to pray for the couple. But as a footballer at the time church was really not my thing. The only prayer I knew, for example, was "Our Father who art in heaven". But this occasion required a different kind of prayer. So I was really scared. But I took on the challenge and I allowed the Holy Spirit to lead me. That day I prayed like I have never prayed before, I tell you, and afterwards people walked up to me to congratulate me on such a wonderful prayer. To this day I still thank God for granting me such wisdom and courage,' he recalled.

But I find Buti Themba's recollections, like my mother's, somewhat underwhelming, especially when it comes to the details about what my father did on the football field for his memory to still enjoy such reverence amongst his peers.

The closest I got to experiencing the magic of Professor Snow

A FATHER IS BORN

White at work was at a football game between Sechaba Primary School and another school at the open grounds close to Kwa-Thema stadium. It was in the early 1990s, and I had tagged along to the game because he was the coach and a teacher at Sechaba. The opposing team was good. They were one up and they kept the Sechaba boys with their backs against the wall for most of the game. In fact, they were running circles around them. My father was beside himself, shouting instructions from the sidelines. But in a last-minute surge for a goal the Sechaba boys were awarded a penalty. My father quickly huddled up with the boys. He told Moremi, a destroyer, to take the spot kick. Moremi had quite a strike in him. Out of all the boys he was the only one who could kick the ball with the fierceness of an Albert 'Bashin' Mahlangu.

'Gents, this is our only chance to level matters,' he said to them. 'Now listen to me carefully, Moremi, I don't want you to try to do anything fancy. I don't want you to try to beat the goalie by kicking the ball to the left or to the right or to the corners of the posts. I just want you to run up as fast as you can to the ball and to kick it as hard as you can straight to the goalie. That's it. But lean forward when you do it because if you lean backwards then there's a high chance that you might balloon the ball. Just be direct,' he said.

After that pep talk Moremi took the ball and he placed it on the penalty spot.

There was some jeering from the other side, but Moremi was now focused. His eyes were fixed and determined. He stood a few paces away from the ball. The referee blew his whistle. Moremi made for the ball and he kicked it hard and straight as he was instructed, and the goalie, instead of standing his ground, ducked to the one side. The molten-hot ball flew between the netless goalposts and landed some metres away from the pitch. Like a hero who had just saved the day, Moremi was hoisted up on the shoulders of his teammates. It was a draw.

A FATHER IS BORN

From that day onwards I had so much respect for my father when it came to all things football. His instruction to Moremi was so simple and yet it was so effective. Here was a man who clearly knew what he was talking about.

Even though I never got the chance to see him in action I'd say that his football story at least was about passion, love and friendship and about the mentoring of young boys into men.

It was my mother who would help him discover his second love – teaching – after his football aspirations came to an end because of a knee injury.

In her novel *The God of Small Things* Arundhati Roy frames the character of Rahel as curious, free-spirited, unintentionally troublesome, something of an indifferent wanderer casually drifting

from one situation to the next. When Larry, an American PhD student, first encounters her as a student at the college of architecture in Delhi he is struck by her casual sense of dress, her wild and curly hair, her gleaming diamond nose-stud, her 'absurdly beautiful collarbones' and her 'nice athletic run'. *There goes a jazz tune*, he thinks to himself, instantly besotted. They fall in love, they get married and they move to America together. But ultimately, their marriage disintegrates just as quickly as it began.

So 'There goes a jazz tune' in a sense is also a euphemism for 'There goes trouble'. It's a bittersweet melody, a chord so discordant it's actually music, with the low notes as intense as the high notes, and I'd like to believe that my mother was one such a 'jazz tune' in my father's life, but a good kind of 'jazz tune' or trouble, I should say, and one that would last him a lifetime almost. She was that fire, that catalyst, that much-needed spark that would ignite in him a desire to be more in life, to pursue more and to dream more.

The two met in 1973, at an inter-high sports weekend. He was doing his Form 4 (now Grade 11) in Tlakula and she was doing Form 3 (Grade 10) in Phulong at the time. He spotted her walking down the street with her little brother, Butinyana. He whistled for her to stop, and as he approached, sweaty in his soccer clothes, Butinyana told her to just agree with everything that he said.

"Whatever he says to you, just say yes, OK?' Butinyana advised.

My mother felt a little uneasy but played it cool. She was looking smart on that day, in a black outfit with a white bow tie which she usually wore for debating. So that helped to ease her anxiety.

'*Heita!*' said my father.

'Hello,' she said, hesitant and careful not to make eye contact.

'*O mang?*' He asked her name.

'*Ke* Nkele,' she said.

'*Awa cava nna ke mang* – Do you know who I am?'
She shook her head.
'*Ke nna* Snowy,' he said, full of himself.
'OK,' she responded.
'I've been watching you for a while now,' he claimed.
But she just nodded, still careful not to make eye contact.
He jumped straight in and asked her for a date.
'OK,' she said, offhandedly.
'So I'll see you later at the soccer game?'

When she told Butinyana that she had agreed to date him he was so excited.

'Wow, I can't wait to tell everybody that Snowy is my new brother-in-law,' he said.

Later on in the afternoon, when she met up with him at the soccer field, she saw what the fuss what about. 'He was the most handsome guy around, like a young Marvin Gaye, a very skilful soccer player, popular, and everybody liked him,' she told me.

Their dating involved going to the bioscope every now and then, going to the open grounds close to Kwa-Thema stadium to watch a soccer game or just hanging out at her house and listening to music all day long in the lounge, which was called the 'dating room', next to the TV room.

'*Mkhulu* didn't want us mixing with boys in the streets,' my mother explained. Instead her father allowed his daughters to bring their boyfriends over to the house so he could keep an eye on them.

'He once even gave your father a few good smacks for coming to the house dressed in his usual Pantsula-style clothes: a *spoti* – a cotton bucket hat – on his head, checked flannel shirt, three-quarter-sized khaki pants and All Star takkies on his feet. *Mkhulu* thought that he was not looking gentlemanly at all for his daughter and so he felt that he needed to correct that. It worked because after that episode your father always made sure that he was appropriately dressed whenever he came to visit.'

My mother remembers him being such a looker that she constantly found herself having to fend off all these girls who were always vying for his attention.

By 1976 they were considering marriage. My father was now working as a dispatch clerk at Van Leer, a metal container plant in Springs. He was a rising 21-year-old man-about-town who was into fashionable clothes and jazz LPs. My mother had just completed her Form 5 (Grade 12) the previous year in Qwa-Qwa in what was then the Orange Free State, and she was now training as a nurse at the Tembisa Hospital. After completing her training, she found work at the East Rand Hospital in Springs. Life was good for the young couple.

But their wedding plans had to be put on hold when my mother fell pregnant.

'Back then there were no clinics in Kwa-Thema to assist women with delivering their babies,' I remember my father saying. 'There were only midwives who would come to your house, and no males whatsoever were allowed in the room when a woman was giving birth.'

On the day that Tshepo was born – 7 August 1977 – my father was not allowed to even stand outside the house. He stood at the corner and waited patiently for someone to let him know what had happened. When someone finally popped out and signalled that everything was OK and that it was a boy he just walked back home. He only got to see Tshepo a couple of days later.

My father was ecstatic about the birth of his firstborn son, and rightly so. But I still doubt that at the age of 21 he fully comprehended how dramatically his life would change. It's often said that when a child is born, so too is the mother. But I think the saying should also extend to men because when a child is born, then so too is the father.

After Tshepo was born my mother insisted that they fast-

A FATHER IS BORN

track their marriage plans, lest my father change his mind. So, on 27 May 1978, the two got married at the Kwa-Thema Methodist Church. On the day my mother wore a white, long-sleeved, tight-fitting, mermaid gown with white gloves, and my father wore a white tux, a black shirt, a big, white bow tie and black trousers. The wedding celebrations spanned two days. It started at the *makoti*'s house – the bride's house – which was my mother's home in Malaza Street in Masimini section of Kwa-Thema, and ended at the *mkhwenyana*'s house, which was my father's home in Nhlengetwa Street, also in Masimini section. The shindig saw the wedding troupe changing into four different outfits, and

A FATHER IS BORN

judging by their wedding pictures I'd say that it was a wonderful affair that was attended by all and sundry.

After the wedding, following the traditional dictates of the time, my mother moved in with my father's family in Nhlengetwa so she could learn more of the ways and the customs of the Mashabas. The important pieces of the puzzle were now in place. But my mother was not yet done.

While she was happy that my father was stepping up as a man and that he was taking care of his responsibilities, she was still adamant that his weekly wages at Van Leer were not enough to secure them a decent future. While my father felt that having a steady job at the factories that paid him his weekly wages was all he needed to be a father and to raise a family, my mother kept impressing upon him that he needed to study for a Primary Teacher's Certificate.

'I told him not to worry about our month-to-month expenses. I assured him that my nursing wages would keep us afloat. I told him that he must just go back to school. That way he can at least get his foot into the teaching profession,' she told me.

My father was a product of Bantu education, an apartheid education system that was designed to make 'hewers of wood and drawers of water' out of black children. It was a system designed only to equip the black child for the unskilled labour market. To some extent I think that this inferior education system did manage to turn my father into a good native somewhat – someone who readily accepted his situation and the limitations set out for him by the apartheid government. My father was no rabble-rouser or agitator. He was no struggle hero. He was just a man who wanted to look after his family and go on about his business. He was not political at all, even though he was brought up in a highly politicised world.

Lending credence to my assertion is his dompas, or pass book, which we found buried deep amongst his personal belongings a couple of months after he died. The brown vinyl-covered dompas was still in pristine condition. Its pages were neither dog-eared nor yellowed by the passage of time. The stamps of approval from the Bantu Affairs Administration Board show him to have been a man who always honoured his mandatory 'check-ins'. These check-ins were basically used as a tool by the government to keep the black population under control. They tracked one's movements, academic pursuits and employment history, amongst other activities. I believe for apartheid to have worked as well as it did for so many years it also needed a great deal of compliance on the part of those that were directly and adversely affected by it, and I believe my father and to a large extent his father, Tshungwane, were such complying natives.

On 25 January 1979 my father finally resigned at Van Leer. In April of 1979 he began his Primary Teacher's Certificate studies at the Hebron Teacher Training College in Mabopane, a rural village that formed part of the Bophuthatswana homeland. My mother continued with her nursing, took care of Tshepo and played her *makoti* role exceptionally well, even going as far as to help my father's younger brother *Rrangwane* Mbuti with his maths homework. She bought my father clothes and she made sure that he always had food and some pocket money.

I do believe my father's eyes were opened when he went to Hebron to do his teacher training course. The education system in Mabopane and other parts of Bophuthatswana was run by the government of Kgosi Lucas Mangope, the President of Bophuthatswana. It can be argued that Mangope, as a homeland leader, wanted an education system that would truly liberate his people. During the early years of independence between 1977 and 1994 great progress was made in building schools and training centres, introducing primary school examinations and creating new high schools and colleges of education. Between 1977 and 1986 the number of primary school children increased from 335 579 to 350 723, while teachers increased from 5 606 to 8 153 — dropping the ratio of learners to teachers from 60:1 to 40:1. By 1985 there were 272 early learning centres, attended by 21 283 children. The number of adult education centres rose from one in 1976 to 173 in 1983. Formal training centres, called manpower centres, were also put in place, offering certification and apprentice training.[7]

So I would say that it was a system indeed designed to uplift the black child, instead of preparing him or her to be a 'hewer of wood' or a 'drawer of water', and I would like to believe that this type of socialisation had quite an impact on my father's life. I think that's where he really started to think differently about himself and what he wanted to be in life.

But it was also in Mabopane that my father, a married man, somehow forgot that he was a married man, when he found himself a girlfriend there. When my mother discovered the affair, she was livid. She tore up all of his fashionable clothes and she threatened to leave the marriage. *Rrangwane* Mbuti says he managed to convince her otherwise. But I think that my mother stayed because she felt that she had invested way too much in the marriage already to let some loose girl take her place. But this was not to be the last time my father strayed, and his infidelities would ultimately play a major part in my parents' divorce.

About two years later, in 1981, my father attained his Primary Teacher's Certificate from Hebron, making him the first person in his family to achieve such a feat. He then worked for a company called Fibreglass Ltd for a short while before he was appointed as a level one teacher at what was then Sechaba Higher Primary School in Kwa-Thema. His appointment came in March 1981, exactly 20 days before his 26th birthday. I think his time in Hebron

---

[7] *A Nation on the March* edited by Dixon Soule Associates, Hans Strydom Publishers (Bophuthatswana) Ltd, 1987.

also went a long way towards honing his Setswana because after being appointed as a level one teacher it didn't take him long to become a fully fledged Setswana teacher.

My father was actually never one for academia, never a natural student or educator, in the way he had been a natural soccer player. For example, when he was working as a level one teacher he also pursued his Senior Education Certificate on the side, but his results were rather unflattering, I must say. He got a D symbol for history; E symbols for Tswana A, Afrikaans second language HG and English B; and F symbols for geography and biology. But by the time he reached the zenith of his teaching career, my father had achieved a significant number of qualifications, ultimately attaining his Bachelor of Education (Honours) degree through the Rand Afrikaans University in 2005.

My mother reckons that if it hadn't been for her insistence that he pursue teaching as a profession, then my father would have worked at Van Leer as a dispatch clerk indefinitely because that's just the type of person he was back then, a person content with the ordinary, a person who couldn't see beyond his football playing aspirations or beyond the fashionable clothes and the jazz LPs that his meagre wages at the plant could afford him.

'I was just not prepared to settle for an average life. I wanted more out of life and I was determined to get it,' she tells me.

PART 2

5

Curious wonder

A FATHER IS BORN

My arrival on 19 June 1982 meant two things for my parents. One, the family was growing and two, as a consequence of point number one, they now had to move out of Nhlengetwa Street and get a place of their own.

The first house they moved into was in Thema Road in Overline. Overline is a much older section of Kwa-Thema, characterised by row houses that are attached to one another with distinctive round ridges on their roofs. The house that my parents moved into was no ordinary house. It was a small, light blue, two-bedroomed house with a sizable but narrow front lawn that stretched about ten feet from the house to the front gate. It's the first house that my mother's older brother Uncle Zakes bought when he was first starting out in life with his then-wife Makgetwa. It's also the first house that my mother's older sister Aunty Dolly moved into with her husband Conference when they were starting out. My mother's younger sister Aunty Dorcas and her then-husband Bushy first moved in after my folks had had their fair share of it, and Uncle Zakes' eldest daughter Reneilwe, commonly known as Toy, also lived there when she was starting out as a young adult. So, the Overline house has been in the family for over four decades and counting.

Unfortunately, I don't have any of my own memories of Overline as a child. Apparently I was a very talkative baby who used to crawl up to the front gate of the house to greet anyone and everyone who passed by. 'Hello ... Hello ... Hello ...' I would incessantly greet people, all day long, until my folks came home from work in the afternoon. I think some passers-by probably thought I was not all there. I'm also told that the lady who used to look after me while my parents were at work was a heavy drinker who dropped me on my head a few times because of her drunken ways. My parents suspect that she even gave me a taste of her choice brew from time to time to put me to sleep. If any passer-by did think I was not all there it was probably her fault.

About three years later my parents bought themselves their very first house in Goede Beste section, or Goede for short. My mother had now transitioned from nursing to teaching and was lecturing in accounting and auditing at the Springs College satellite campus in Kwa-Thema next to the Habedi police station. Tshepo was doing Sub B (Grade 2) at Canon Rakale Primary School and I was going to Kwa-Thema Crèche (the university of crèches in Kwa-Thema) in Kataza Street. In the afternoons my father's eldest niece, Barbara, would look after us until our parents came back home from work.

This new housing development project in Goede catered for black professionals such as teachers, nurses and policemen and women. They were the first 'bonded' homes in Kwa-Thema. Our house was number 11341 on Ndlovu Street. It was a cream-white two-bedroomed house with a kitchen, a small lounge, a bathroom with a toilet, a detached garage and a small backyard, which at the time I thought was huge. From the foundation up, these cluster houses were stunningly modern. They had gable roofs with clay tiles and some were face-brick, while others, like our house, were cement-plastered. Our street, peculiarly, was left untarred by the municipality after construction and there was no drainage system to speak of. It would flood profusely whenever it rained, which was either a good or a bad thing for us kids, depending on what type of street games we wanted to play on that particular rainy day.

Back then, time was forever. Tshepo and I used to run amok in the streets. The house next to our house had the municipal 'danger' – an orange-coloured electrical substation – right in front of it. The 'danger' was a meeting point for all the neighbourhood kids. So we didn't have to go far to find friends. We literally had to walk out of the gate and the other kids would be there. We played all sorts of games, sometimes even long after the sun had set. Sometimes we played *bafana to mantombazane* – 'boys versus girls', and sometimes we had mashed-up teams, young and old, boys and girls. We played games like tag; *skop-die-bal*, a hide-and-seek game that involved kicking a ball to knock down cans that were stacked up on each other; 'stinie', a game similar to America's version of hopscotch; marbles; and *diketo*, a coordination game with marbles or small stones. In this game the players scoop up a specified number of small stones from little dug-out holes in the ground. You have to do this while throwing one stone into the air, scooping the rest of the stones out of the holes with one hand before catching the falling stone. We also played 'one *pali*' – soccer with just one brick as the goalpost – and *moraba-raba*, a traditional board game.

Behind the Goede homes was *is'ganga* – a bit of veld – where we often played soccer. There we hunted down *imbiba* – rodents – by flushing them out of their holes using litres and litres of water fetched in bottles. Sometimes we made catties or slingshots by cutting up tree branches and old tyre tubes, and used them to shoot down birds. We would make a fire to braai whatever rodent we had caught or whatever bird we had shot down. One of us would be sent home to steal an egg, another to steal a potato, and another to steal some bread or cooking oil or salt. Then we'd have ourselves a mini feast right there at the veld. We also used to jump on old, worn out mattresses there. I used to fancy myself a gymnast in those days, and I must say that I was pretty good. I knew all the moves: the cartwheel, the fall-flat, the side spin, the backflip and the front flip.

At the north end of the veld was a mine dump which had morphed into a mountain of sharp-edged granite rocks over the years. We used to slide down that mountain of a mine dump using scrap metal sheets, as one would ski down a snow-covered mountain. Obviously this dangerous practice happened unbeknown to our parents.

Another place that we were constantly warned against was the graveyard just across from the veld. But we went there in any case. It was our treasure trove, our adventure place and a route to and from Five Chuck – an abandoned building behind the mine dump that looked like a derelict beer hall. It had a dead-bolted water supply where kids like us used to swim. Recently I learnt that 'Five Chuck' was actually built for mineworkers around the 1960s and that it was actually called Five Shaft because it had five shafts. Sangomas used to converge there for their rituals, and stories abounded of kids drowning or disappearing there. But that didn't stop us from going.

Kwa-Thema had a wonderful mix of people who spoke different languages such as Sesotho, isiZulu, Sepedi, isiXhosa and even Afrikaans. Amongst my friends, for example, was Bangane, who spoke isiXhosa; Titi, who spoke Sesotho; the brothers Tshepo and Tsitsi, who spoke Setswana, like us, even though we were Pedi; Linda, who spoke isiZulu; and Isabella, who spoke English, Afrikaans and a bit of isiNdebele. So we grew up speaking many different languages in Kwa-Thema, all thanks to the very same people of Kwa-Thema who, in the 1950s, with the support of the United Party, refused to be separated along tribal lines by the National Party when the first bricks of Kwa-Thema were being laid. In the end the National Party conceded that it was impossible to separate people along their tribal lines in the new township.[8]

Kwa-Thema, like most townships in South Africa, also had its fair share of characters. There was Goli, a no-nonsense, pot-bellied

---

8   Denis, Philippe. *The Dominican Friars in Southern Africa: A Social History (1577–1990)*. Studies in Christian Mission, Vol.21, 1998. Leiden: Brill.

speed cop. He was a mean guy. He would give you a speeding ticket for riding your bicycle fast, or if he didn't like the way you were riding your bicycle in general, he would give you some other fine. In our minds, as kids, those speeding tickets or fines were real. There was also Maggie, a feisty, tough-natured lady with dwarfism. She was a novelty in the township, a spectacle, but one who didn't look for handouts and who didn't want people to feel sorry for her. Maggie went on with her business like everybody else and she always stood up for herself. Kids used to make fun of her whenever they saw her, but she took it all in her stride. I loved her actually. Whenever I saw her, my heart would be filled with wonder and amazement. There was Mandla Magalai, our township magician, who did all sorts of tricks for 50 cents a pop. He made things disappear and reappear right before our very eyes. He also did card tricks. Every time we'd see him approach we'd run inside the house to ask for 50 cents and then we'd run back out again in excitement. But it always ended so quickly – the trick, that is – and Mandla was firm. It did not matter how much we begged him to do another trick, if you didn't have 50 cents then he was on his way again.

Maizuzu was a homeless man who lived in a rubbish dump all by himself. He was a scary figure, always covered in dirty, tattered rags. Parents used to scare their kids with the threat of Maizuzu. 'I'll give you to Maizuzu if you don't want to listen,' or 'Maizuzu will come and get you,' they used to say. One day my cousin Bongane was lost and they couldn't find him anywhere. Panic set in as the adults searched for him. After some hours of searching, they found him safe and sound and chilling with Maizuzu at the dumpsite nearby. There was Meneer Hosea, a perpetual drunk of a teacher who taught at Sechaba Primary School, and who was my father's peer. He didn't have a wife, but he had two boys, Tshepo and Thabang. He was the kind of drunk who would pee himself whenever he was in that state, and then wobble back home for hours on end. A five-minute walk from his favourite watering hole back to his home would take him hours. We used to make fun of him as children, but the grown-ups were rather solemn about his situation.

What would any township be without that gangster fellow and his crew of thugs who terrorised everyone? Ours was a fellow named Moya, whom I'd never seen with my own two eyes. Or maybe I did but I just didn't know it was him. I'm told that Moya was a nice, handsome lad who unfortunately turned to a life of crime and gangsterism somewhere along the way. Legend has it that his mother was a sangoma and that she gave him *amabande*, muti-laced straps, to make him invincible. Moya apparently wore those straps on both of his arms. He had the reputation of being a mean driver. Moya, as his name suggested, had a knack for disappearing right into thin air whenever the police were in hot pursuit of him. A typical car chase would see Moya driving into an open soccer field and spinning his Cressida: like a tornado he would raise up dust with his spinning to confuse the police before disappearing into thin air again. It was said that it was his sangoma mother who gave him the powers to disappear like that.

I was from a well-to-do family with two working professionals, both teaching, and two well-behaved children to complete the picture. My parents were aspirational, educated, stylish, beautiful and young. They were determined to succeed in life, and they were also determined to make us a good home. My parents didn't touch alcohol and there was no nonsensical 'father chasing the mother down the streets' type of fight in our house. Their standards were very high, and as a reflection of them we had to look just as good, be just as prim and proper and just as well-mannered as they were. My mother always made sure that we were clean and manicured, that we had no 'jam in our ears' and that we ate well. On Sunday mornings we would wash up and go to our local Evangelical Lutheran Church, just as my paternal grandmother always stressed that we should do.

On Christmas Day we always got new clothes. That's how our parents showed affection to us. Our parents, like many other black parents at the time, never said, 'I love you,' and they never displayed their feelings openly, be it to us or to each other, especially in public. We only saw the 'I love yous' and the 'hugs and the kisses goodnight' on TV. I don't know why, but in most black families a show of affection like that was just an alien concept.

As teachers, my parents kept us well supplied with educational toys such as Scrabble, building blocks, abacuses, crayons and drawing books. They liked us to read books like the *Once upon a Time* collection of short stories and Enid Blyton's The Secret Seven series. But we also had some fun toys, such as Monopoly, drafts, snakes and ladders, cards and play cars. I had a toy silver cowboy gun which I got from a lucky packet, and a see-through water gun – though I had wanted a toy machine gun that flickered and made loud shooting noises instead. We also had a big moveable swimming pool, the only one in the neighbourhood, and as a consequence our house was usually the mecca for all the neighbourhood kids during the spring and the summer months.

My toy laptop computer was a real asset to me because it helped me to learn about the world around me. I knew about astronauts and how the Earth rotated on its own axis way before I learnt about those things at school. One day, while we were watching some TV game show, the quizmaster asked one of the contestants what the famous wall in China was called. 'The Great Wall!' I blurted out. My father looked at me as if I were crazy, and shook his head. After a few seconds while both he and the contestant tried to figure out the right answer, the quizmaster hit the buzzer and told them that time was up. The answer was 'The Great Wall'. My father was stunned. I looked at him. But he just kept his eyes trained on the TV, a frown on his face.

But my most treasured play item was my *driewiel*, a red three-wheeler with a big front wheel with pedals and two smaller wheels at the back. That three-wheeler initiated me into the simple pleasures that come with being able to physically propel an object from point A to point B. I remember how I used to bully my father out of the passageway with my red tricycle and how I used to order him to come wipe my bum when I was done with my business in the toilet. I was not scared of him in those early days.

My imagination was wild and free back then. I was always talking about this or the other to anyone who would listen, and my father would indulge me with a smile. I really was a loud-mouth. I would talk and talk and Tshepo would be so annoyed. I remember my brother at this stage as a quiet, calm child. He was handsome and athletic, and he had an enigmatic personality that had everyone gravitating towards him. I was the chubby, talkative younger brother. But it wasn't just the talking that annoyed him. Once my father bought us matching but different-coloured shiny Kappa tracksuits, and for a while we were known as the 'Kappa boys' or the '*Robe di Kappa* boys' in the neighbourhood. Tshepo hated it and he hated matching up with me even more. But I didn't mind. I thought it was cool.

Back then kids could wander about without their parents worrying about their safety. I could spend almost the whole day away from home and come back only to fix myself a sandwich and then be off again. It was on one such quiet and peaceful day that it became apparent to me that I was in fact a unique human being and that there was only one of me in the entire world. I was probably wandering about in the backyard or sitting under the shade of a tree or just lounging under the shade cast by our house and looking up at the clear blue skies when this dawned on me. I was probably four years old. The idea that I was in total control of my being and of this body that I was occupying was an epiphany. I was my own person and there was no copy of me out there. I was Tumiso. At that young age I was alive to the uniqueness of my existence, and of my inner voice, which I could hear crystal clear without even mouthing a single word. The experience fostered the introspective side of me. To this day I still enjoy time on my own, just me and my thoughts.

When I was around five or six years old my father bought me a red and white two-wheeler. I rode that bike on training wheels until my mother's eldest nephew, Phondo, who is actually my big brother in African terms, visited us one day. Phondo felt that those training wheels were making me a *bari* – a fool of note – and so he took them off. He told me to get on the bike and to hit the road, while he guided me from behind.

'*Tjova!* – Put some umpf in it!' he kept coaching me.

I wobbled. I fell. I scratched my knees. I crashed into walls and I cried my eyes out. But in the end I could ride that bicycle without any training wheels. I went everywhere with that bike. It was my Kitt and I was its Michael Knight.

The first memory I have of my father, the 'strange man', is when I left this bike unattended on Motlhaping Street. We had been told countless times to never play there.

'Just play here on Ndlovu Street where we can see you,' they used to say.

I had friends in Motlhlaping. So invariably I would find my way there somehow. But my father couldn't know. My mother was easy, but not my father. I had to be very sneaky if I wanted to play there and I had to make sure that I was back home before he came back from work or from soccer training. On that particular day I was having way too much fun. But then the rain clouds suddenly gathered, and the heavy winds blew dust all over the place.

Everyone dashed for cover. It was in the excitement and the scatter that I forgot my bicycle.

When he got home, my father asked where my bicycle was. I said that it was in the garage. He shook his head. He grabbed me by the hand, and he dragged me out of the house. On our way to Motlhaping he kept whacking my back with his open hand, his other hand tightly gripping my arm so I couldn't break free.

'Why *o bua maka*? Why *o bua maka*? – Why are you lying? Why are you lying?' he kept on asking, while whacking my back black and blue. He let up when we got to the passageway that connected Goede section and Motlhaping.

I was crying hysterically. He put me up on his shoulders and he started smacking me on the legs when we got to Motlhaping. I turned my head and I saw my bicycle lying on the ground, abandoned, with dust particles blowing around it, and it hit me that I had forgotten the bike there.

My father let me down and he grabbed the bicycle. 'What is this? What is this?' he asked, and he whacked me some more.

I know that he was upset at my negligence. I know that he wanted me to be more careful and attentive with my things. I know that he was more upset about me leaving my bike there on the side of the road as if I was some rich spoilt kid whose parents could just buy him another one than he was about me playing at Motlhaping Street.

But the punishment was excessive for a five- or six-year-old. I had never seen my father this angry. I now saw him at his worst. It wasn't a wild outburst. It was a controlled, sustained kind of anger. He knew exactly what he was doing.

I was changed after that. I became withdrawn. Careful. Calculating. I became a child who wasn't really a child. Self-doubt crept in and I just couldn't shake it off. It became a part of me, a part of my being, a scar. The sting of his open hand took away the joy of being carefree, of discovering the world around me with no inhibitions and with no fear.

Interactions with my father were never quite the same. I approached and spoke to him with caution.

I lost something that day. But so too did he. I was scarred, but so was he.

6

The strange man

When I began my Standard 1 (now Grade 3) in 1990 at Sechaba Primary School I quickly learnt that physical punishment was something that was meted out not just at home but also at school. It was completely acceptable. For example, the teaching style at Sechaba, as in most township schools at the time, was recitation-based. The teacher would write on the chalkboard, point to it with a cane and say whatever was written there. And then the class, in a chorus, would repeat after him, all day long. That's actually how we learnt vowels.

Teacher: A, E, I, O, U
Learners: A, E, I, O, U
Teacher: Ma, me, mi, mo, mu.
Learners: Ma, me, mi, mo, mu.
Teacher: Ba, be, bi, bo, bu.
Learners: Ba, be, bi, bo, bu ... and so on.
With mathematics it was the same thing.
Teacher: One plus one is two.
Learners: One plus one is two.
Teacher: Two plus two is four.
Learners: Two plus two is four.

If some learners did not repeat what the teachers were saying, like the good parrots they should have been, then the cane would be used for something entirely other. We were never really taught how one arrives at two or how one arrives at four. All we had to do was to repeat after the teacher and memorise that information. But the problem with this kind of learning was that once we were out of the classroom, so too was the lesson from our heads. The lessons were not committed to our memories through a sustained process of understanding what made sense. Instead, we were taught in a repetitive, 'mimicry' style of teaching, and always with a cane in hand.

Corporal punishment really was part and parcel of the education system. A whack of the cane on the bum and on the hands was frequently dished out by the teachers for any kind of transgression. Some teachers went overboard. It was as if they were taking their frustrations out on us. Our classroom teacher, Mr Msiza, was one such teacher. He was a tall, lanky fellow who kept his nails long so he could pinch us if we didn't listen to him during his maths lessons. He used his long nails to pinch the tender part of our ears. He would also sometimes use his long nails to pinch a girl's inner thigh, which was rather perverted and sadistic when I think about it now.

But some teachers were nice and never laid a hand on any learner, like the fair-skinned, slit-eyed and white-haired Borife Raborife, who still stands as Sechaba's longest-serving principal, after taking over the reins from Mr Molapo (the school's first principal when it was founded back in 1965), the bespectacled and ever-smiling Joyce Ncokazi and the feisty but loving Dorah Mohapi. And Meneer Sekgapane. Meneer Sekgapane, in my opinion, was simply a class act and a cut above the rest. He stands out for me as a teacher who broke the mould when it came to teaching.

He was a dark-skinned man with big round eyes, blemishes on his cheeks that some say were due to his excessive intake of the hot stuff, and yellowed fingertips from his habit of chain-smoking cigarettes. He was an all-rounder, who taught many subjects at the school. He was an excellent orator, a dramatist who could paint pictures with his words. He knew when to pause for effect and when to up the pace for suspense. Watching him in action was like watching a flying trapeze show unfolding right before your very eyes. He was authoritative, but not in the 'I'm the teacher and you are the student so you will listen to me,' kind of way. He had a calm, confident power about him. He didn't have to impose his power. It was just there.

He instilled confidence in each of us because he made us believe that we could achieve anything in life as long as we put education at the centre. His classes were always lively, interactive and raucous with laughter. Some lessons, he would ask us to come up to the front and share stories with our classmates off the top of our heads. My chubby friend, Neo, always came out tops with this exercise because like Meneer Sekgapane he was a natural storyteller with a creative imagination. While other teachers were preoccupied with getting us to cram things word for word, Meneer Sekgapane was more concerned with our minds, our imaginations and our self-confidence.

Sadly, my father, young as he was, belonged to the group of teachers who believed in corporal punishment as a way of getting through to the learners. At school he had a reputation for being a neat and snazzy dresser with an enviable collection of ties and shoes. On the surface he was a natural charmer with that sheepish smile of his, his Afro and his unkempt full beard from the disco era. His energy as a young teacher was boundless. For example, Sechaba, being the township school that it was, had no intercoms, so whenever there was an urgent message my father would volunteer. He would go from class to class, delivering the message, making light fun of the students while at it. But he also had the reputation of being a strict, no-nonsense teacher whose open-hand and backhand smacks were a force to be reckoned with. They were forceful, nerve-shattering.. No one ever saw them coming. He was a man who was easily riled up, so if he came across some Pantsula chap who thought he knew too much then a lightning fast smacking wouldn't be too far off. It was a disarming, disorienting experience. While you were still explaining yourself ... then THWAA! His *warm klap* would rattle you off your feet.

And sadly for us – Tshepo and me – it was at home where this side of him would find the most expression.

———

One incident I clearly remember is the 'Coca-Cola bottle' incident. Wednesdays and Fridays were fish-and-chips or takeaway nights at home and I always looked forward to them. This Wednesday my father had decided to throw Coca-Cola into the mix. He took an empty one-litre Coke bottle and threw me over his shoulders, and we went to the shops together. We came back with a full new bottle of Coca-Cola. I was wildly excited. My father loved Coke with all his heart. It was his favourite drink.

When we got home he placed the bottle on the kitchen floor while he attended to something. I don't know why, but in my excitement I decided that this was an opportune time for me to practise my breakdancing moves. Prophets of Da City, South Africa's first hip-hop group, had just released their first album *Our World* and it was all the rage in our neighbourhood. They were all about emceeing on the microphone, deejaying on the decks, breakdancing and spray painting grafitti on the walls, and even though I was into Bruce Lee and Michael Jackson, I found their music videos magnetic. So naturally I fancied myself a breakdancer.

I kept doing the 'one leg sweep' move on the floor. My father told me to cut it out. But I just kept on doing it until ... BOOM! I knocked over the Coca-Cola bottle. It shattered and the foamy drink splashed all over the kitchen floor. My father, livid, smacked me on my face with his open hand so hard that I immediately fell, dizzy and shaken. There was a buzzing tone in my ears. And like a gushing faucet, I just let loose in my short pants. Then it was one, two, more whacks on the back. I wanted to cry out loud, but my father told me not to because he had warned me and I just hadn't listened. So, I whimpered instead. Tears flooded down my face but I withheld my usual noisy crying lest I get another smack on the face.

He went for the mop and the scoopy and told me to not move an inch because there was shattered glass all over the place. I just stood there, whimpering, my short pants soaking wet, my face red-hot and buzzing. It was the worst pain and shame I had ever felt. Tshepo looked at me sorrowfully. I wanted to go to my room and cry in peace without his stares, without someone feeling sorry for me. I wanted to be alone. But I had to stand there and wait for my father to finish cleaning the mess that I had made. After a while, my tears dried into salty lines on my face.

When he had finished cleaning up the mess, he told me to go to my room and change. I don't know if he ever went back to the shops to buy another bottle of Coke – his much beloved soft drink – but that day I stopped tagging along with him to the shops. Some years later, doctors would tell him to cut out Coke completely from his diet because of his diabetes. The irony still astounds me.

To be smacked around like that takes away something from a person, let alone a child. You become just an object. You cease to be human. That does something to a person. I hated and I blamed myself for being this object that could be so easily smacked and whacked around.

―――

I had never been a bed-wetter before, but when the smacking and the whacking became more commonplace I started wetting my bed at night. For my father it was completely unacceptable that I was in primary school and was still wetting my bed, and the smacks I would get for my bed-wetting were really bad. I was always scared when morning came. It was tormenting trying to hide the wet sheets or to disguise the urine stench on my clothes. Sometimes I would pee right before bed, but I would still wind up peeing myself at night. Sometimes I even went along with the big boys on their rodent hunt missions in the veld across the way because I was told that if I ate the meat from a rodent then I would stop bed-wetting for sure. It didn't work.

On top of it, I was a thumbsucker. So I was given a hard time on two fronts, for my bed-wetting and for my thumbsucking. I felt so ashamed. Ashamed of my bed-wetting, ashamed of my thumbsucking and ashamed of the hidings and the talking-tos that I would get as a result of it all. I felt trapped in this cycle of bed-wetting, thumbsucking, trying to hide the two, getting caught and getting a beating. I felt as if I would never get out of this horrible movie that I was living in, a movie that was on constant replay.

Playing in the streets became my only respite. There I was free to suck my thumb to my heart's content and if I had an accident in my short pants I could just wait it out until they were dry before I went back home.

At some point my father stopped giving me hidings for my bed-wetting, but the psychological torture persisted. When he stopped the frequent whacking and smacking, his voice – angry, unpredictable – became his new weapon of choice. I could never get used to it: the tone and volume gave me a fright every time. It did not matter what he had to say. He could be giving me a compliment, but I would automatically wet myself when I heard it. And if it wasn't his voice it was his presence. His aura was negative. Nothing really impressed him. He didn't even laugh properly. His laugh was more of a sarcastic chuckle.

To Tshepo and me he was this one-dimensional being who was always on the lookout for mistakes. My brother and I stayed in our room most of the time: we played there and talked to each other there until our mother would call us out to come eat and to watch TV. She was the neutraliser of the tension between us and our father. We loved having her around. She made everything better, albeit for a little while. Sometimes when we were holed up in our room my father would stand by the door without us even knowing he was there.

I remember one day when Tshepo and I were playing in our

room. We didn't have action figures, so we used Lego blocks to make up our own characters and then we'd have play fights with the Lego blocks. While we were playing and talking, Tshepo suddenly said 'Shhh ...' and he placed his index finger against his lips, signalling me to hush. I was perplexed, but I kept my mouth shut. He pointed to the door, which was open just a crack. He got up from the floor, crept slowly to the door and quickly opened it. Lo and behold, my father was right there, standing behind the door. He was shocked that he had been caught out listening in on us. Tshepo went to the toilet to take a leak and my father went casually off to rejoin my mother in the TV room.

This 'strange man' had now truly become a permanent resident in our house and he was not going anywhere.

The whole thing was so creepy. I don't know how much of our conversation he had heard. I was terribly uneasy because Tshepo and I spoke about everything. We would ask ourselves why we were being treated so badly and why we'd been born. We were honestly not proud to be the Mashaba children, the ones that everyone else outside our home envied. Our parents were both present and they were both teachers, but we still wished for other parents. We wished for parents who weren't as strict.

My mother never really gave us hidings. She would use a slipper or she would give us a half-hearted slap on the buttocks to get us back on track. But that was rare. A good talking-to was what did the trick for her. She left all the 'disciplining' to my father, who in turn ran riot. Maybe at the time she felt that my father was right to have such a heavy hand with us. She probably thought that one needed to be hard and firm to raise boys into men – it was commonly believed in those days. 'Spare the rod and spoil the child,' was one of her favourite lines. But in the meantime, our self-confidence was being shattered, and any sense of family security was fast eroding.

But we relied on and confided in each other as brothers,

because no one knew of our struggles better than us.

I used to tag along with Tshepo all the time. Wherever he was, you could be sure that I was not far off. By then I had graduated to a blue BMX. I saw the world on that bike, exploring Kwa-Thema and all of her surrounds, together with my brother and our friends. We even rode as far as Geluksdal, a coloured township, where there was a public swimming pool for black people. Sometimes on good days, we'd swim. On other days, the coloured boys, who felt the pool was theirs, would fight us. They would chase us away and tell us, '*Gaan by julle mense!* Go to your people!' Tshepo was not afraid of these coloured boys and he would even fight them to make sure that we all got a fair chance to take a dip in the pool. He was my hero.

Tshepo was someone that I looked up to and wanted to become, but he was not above teasing me. The time I remember most clearly occurred when I was around eight years old, when

clashes between the Inkatha Freedom Party (IFP) and the African National Congress (ANC) had turned Kwa-Thema into something of a warzone. The sight of comrades marching and singing struggle songs was commonplace. I admired them and I would raise my fist and shout out 'Viva!' in solidarity with them, but from afar of course. My parents had warned me never to mix with the comrades because they used to 'necklace people' and they also used to 'get beaten up or arrested by the soldiers'.

Movement was difficult during the day and even more difficult at night. In the mornings Inkatha would form blockades to prevent people from going to work in town. In the afternoons they would take people out of the taxis on their way home from work and would do Lord knows what to them. When the police intervened, the IFP moved deeper into the township which was ANC territory. But luckily for my parents they worked within the township and so they could move a little easier than most people during the day.

One day there was an Inkatha threat and our teachers released us earlier than usual. When we got home we locked ourselves in, lest the Inkatha bloodhounds come bursting in and butcher us in the house. We had heard stories of how they would run into people's homes at will and hack everyone with their pangas. My folks were still at work, so it was just me and Tshepo at home. There was not a soul on the streets.

Tshepo decided to play outside, but then he came rushing back in. He locked the door and told me that they were coming, and then he dashed to our room. I just stood there in the kitchen, frozen, not knowing what to do. I peed myself a little. I then made for the kitchen drawer. I pulled out a butcher's knife. I lifted my T-shirt and I directed the point of the knife just below my stomach. I waited patiently for someone to burst in through the kitchen door. That would be my cue to plunge the knife deep into my stomach. At eight years of age, I figured that taking my own life was probably much better than being hacked to death by those bloodthirsty bastards. I waited. My hands were shaking. I was trembling. I thought of my mother and I thought of my father and of the pain they would feel if they came home only to find us hacked to death in the house. My whole life played out before my very eyes. I swear.

Then Tshepo came up from behind me and said '*Heyi wena!* What are you doing? I'm just joking, man. No one is coming.'

He then laughed his heart out. It was a terrible prank. I didn't find it funny at all. That was the first and the last time I ever considered taking my own life.

―

In 1992 my brother and I changed schools. I was sent to Springs Secondary School in Bakerton, a predominantly Indian school, for my Standard 3 (now Grade 5) and Tshepo was sent to Alra Park High School in Nigel, a predominantly coloured school, for his Standard 6 (now Grade 8). My parents, even though they were teachers in township schools, felt that our new schools would be much better for our educational development. The transition was extremely difficult for both of us, primarily because of the language factor. We had to switch from Setswana to English, and even though we could read and write in English we were neither fluent nor even moderately conversant in the language. We just couldn't express ourselves freely in English.

While in Sechaba we had been top students, in these new schools we sank to below average. Springs Secondary School was nothing like Sechaba. They had a swimming pool, double-storey buildings hosting classrooms, big open spaces with well-manicured lawns and plants, soccer, rugby and cricket fields, netball courts, a library, music classrooms, laboratories, a tuck shop, a woodwork classroom and much more. It was an intimidating environment for me from the start, and I'm sure Tshepo felt just as overwhelmed at Alra Park, even though he masked it with his usual 'I fear nothing and no man' bravado.

The first friends I made in this new school were Levine and Llewellyn. They were kind to me. They helped me to acclimatise to the new environment. They even shared their lunch with me from time to time. But the other kids were not so nice. They used to make fun of me, laugh at me behind my back, some even straight to my face. So, I was quiet and I kept to myself most of the time. I spoke only when spoken to, and when I did speak it was with a really low voice because I was not confident in English. Then they would make fun of my quiet tone. Some called me 'stompie nose' because of the shape of my nose. The black kids called me '*mhlathi*' because of my fat cheeks.

My confidence plummeted. In class I felt really stupid. There was no more Meneer Sekgapane to help elevate my self-esteem. I couldn't keep up. At lunch I would ask Levine and Llewellyn to explain to me what the teachers had said. Sometimes they would oblige me, and sometimes they would just run off to play. Sometimes in class I would nod incessantly, as if I understood, but then if the teacher asked me a question I would go blank and the whole class would burst out laughing. Some teachers even called me stupid – *dom* – without batting an eyelid.

There was a girl called Jane Chaka in my class. She was my homegirl in a sense because we lived close to each other back in Kwa-Thema. We were the only two black kids in that class. But Jane had been in this new school for much longer than I had, and she knew her way around. She knew everyone. One would think that she was the ideal person to help me out, but actually she was not. She joined in making fun of me with the rest. Sometimes she would even be the one leading the attack. One day as I was walking into the classroom she pulled down my tracksuit pants and exposed my underwear. I quickly pulled my pants back up. But it was too late. Everyone was in stitches with laughter. Sometimes, as class monitor, she would write my name down on the board for no reason at all, just to get me in trouble – and, mind you, I was the quietest child in that class.

Back home, my father wasn't letting up either. Although he had eased up a bit with the smacking, his psychological onslaught persisted. Every week he would give me an allowance of R5 and I was expected to use that money wisely. In other words, I was expected to save it. But by the first day of the week, that money would be finished, because I would spend it all on sweets and crisps. One of my favourite sweets were the 'black balls' which we called 'nigger balls' – I only realised later how offensive that term was.

I would come back home and make up stories about how I had lost the money. In the beginning he would give me another R5, but he stopped doing that fairly soon. Instead, he began to torment me over my 'reckless' spending habits. He'd have me in the room for what seemed like hours, interrogating me about what I had done with the money and picking out any inconsistencies in my stories. The more I lied or said 'I don't know,' the more I would get smacked.

It weighed heavily on me. Every day after school he would come into our room while we changed into our home clothes and he would ask me about the money. It was like a ritual for him. To this day I don't know why those R5 coins mattered so much to him. But I worried more about what I would say when I came home from school after 'squandering' that R5 than I did about my schoolwork.

So I started visiting my cousin Kgotso over weekends, as a way of getting away from home, and also because he had a handsome coin collection. He used Prestik to stick the coins on a cardboard chart. The first column was for the 10 cent coins, the second for the 20 cent coins, and so on, with the last column being for the R5 coins. He kept this treasure trove under his bed.

While a group of us were watching TV or playing outside, I would pretend that I desperately needed the toilet. I would stand in the passageway between the toilet and Kgotso's bedroom for a second or two, to make sure that the coast was clear. Satisfied, I would go into his room, crouch under his bed and rip out a R2 coin from one column, a R1 coin from another, two 50 cent coins and maybe another R2 coin for good measure, so that he'd think that they probably fell off on their own somewhere on the floor of his room. Or so I thought. Then I would make for the bathroom, where I would flush the toilet and run the basin taps for a few minutes while my nerves settled, before joining everyone else again.

For a while my problems disappeared, because now I had Kgotso's coin collection chart to cover my spending. But Kgotso grew suspicious. He started hiding away the big coins – the R1, the R2 and the R5 coins – and leaving only the useless coins on the chart, which meant that I would have to nick about a hundred to make up the R5. So, it just wasn't worth my time any more. I stopped visiting and I was back to square one.

The result of this R5 coin saga, I'd say, was that I lost my self-pride: I felt that by stealing to appease my father – to try to show him that I could be responsible and not waste money on things like sweets and crisps like other children – I had stooped to a very low level. I hated myself for stealing and I hated the fact that Kgotso now trained his eyes on me like a hawk every time I came to visit because I had turned into this little thief that couldn't be trusted. He didn't accuse me outright, and he didn't have to. I hated myself and I hated my father even more for directly or indirectly putting me in that position.

Back in school I could manage mathematics and art, but I was failing the rest of my subjects dismally. I found joy only in the road-and-rail bridge on the Welgedacht route between Springs and Bakerton, the route to school. It was the very same road-and-rail bridge that my mother as a little girl used to relish whenever they crossed it on the bus during the old Payneville days.

Tshepo's school performance was also suffering. My mother made a point of sitting with us and our books in the kitchen while she was cooking, and that's when it became apparent to me that Tshepo was actually something of a 'slow learner', the term used back then. For example, my mother would ask him to read out loud and he would get stuck on certain words – words that I could say in my mind with absolute ease, like 'through', 'though' and 'thought'. Now I think he was not really a 'slow learner' but he needed some more positive reinforcement and a far less irritable guiding hand than my mother's.

My mother would get so angry with Tshepo and he would just keep hitting a brick wall. Her impatience really affected his confidence, even though he didn't show it. Once she made me read out loud something that he was struggling with.

When I finished reading my mother said, 'You see?' to Tshepo.

I didn't mean to show him up – I was just doing what my mother had instructed me to do. I don't think that she knew the extent of the damage that she was doing. But I know that Tshepo was embarrassed even though he didn't show it. Our relationship was definitely strained after that. A distance grew between us and we were no longer confidants.

This wound festered right before our eyes and neither of us could do anything about it. There was no going back. There was no going forward either. Instead, we stood by and watched the decay.

7

Tshepo

In primary school Tshepo was a football and track and field god. He was actually an all-round phenomenon, diligent with his schoolwork and a marvel to watch on the sporting field. He was born with a naturally athletic body and had these massive Herculean calves to boot.

He was a handsome fellow too. He was fair-skinned and had a slim face, a sharp chin, the most perfect straight-edged nose I had ever seen, a slight gap-toothed smile and dark, full lips that blew thick and full as he grew into his own. To put it in American terms he was a 'jock'. He wore the school's number 10 soccer jersey and he was positioned last to receive the baton in every relay race because of how fast he was. He was an incredible sprinter, the kind that would have the entire school chanting his English name 'Victor! Victor! Victor!' when he took his position behind the starting line. He had all these medals and trophies from his sporting exploits and I wanted to be like him with all of my heart.

By the time he reached high school he wanted to be the next Pelé. But my folks felt the time had come for him to start going to the confirmation class at our Evangelical Lutheran Church. A confirmation class is a four- or six-month training programme for adolescent students who want to learn more about the Christian faith. At the end of this programme they get to be confirmed or to be 'baptised again' in a special ceremony at the church.

Tshepo hated every minute of confirmation class, and it messed up his soccer practice schedule. At the class they had to read religious texts in Latin written by Martin Luther – not the civil rights leader from the United States, but the founder and father of our Christian denomination – and they had to know these Latin texts off by heart by the confirmation ceremony at the end of the year. There were other church-related activities too. He literally had no time to himself. He had no time to be a regular teenager. After school he had to wash his school clothes, help me with mine, prepare us food and get his homework done, and then he had to head straight out to either the confirmation class or soccer practice. Sometimes he would come home late and then my father would start.

'Why are you late? What were you up to all this time?' And the beatings would resume all over again.

As each day passed we grew more and more apart.

In Alra Park he started mixing with a gang who called themselves the Vatos Locos or VLs. Their leader, Tshepo told me, was some dark-skinned, gap-toothed fellow named Ghost. He used to tell me stories of how they would bunk school and hang out at so-and-so's place, how they would smoke, drink and rob kids of their money to buy *slap* chips, how they would mix with all these different girls and how on some days he would run, side by side with his new hero Ghost, from the police who wanted to take them back to school. He had some new friends now and girls were starting to take quite a liking to him. He was blooming into a fine, handsome young man after all, and he naturally entertained these girls.

Back home he would lie about his whereabouts, about why he didn't do this or do that, and my father would, unsurprisingly, try to have another go at him. But he was a teenager who was now coming into his own and soon he stopped crying when my father beat him. He would just zone out until it was all over. He wouldn't dare hit or push my father, but his insolence was palpable. He became passive-aggressive, and I think my father could feel the strength of the young man he was becoming. There was nothing that my father could do because the only way of disciplining he knew was to give hidings.

Once he held on tight to a belt that my mother was whipping him with. My father was not around on that day and she probably felt that it was up to her to take matters into her own hands. She tried with all of her might to pull the belt back, but Tshepo held on to it.

With him getting more and more out of hand, my parents decided that he should stop playing soccer altogether and focus solely on his schoolwork and on the confirmation class. I suppose they were like any other parents who just wanted a good education and Jesus above all else for their children. I also suspect that being a former soccer player himself, one whose dreams had been cut short by a knee injury, my father probably felt that it was best to dissuade him from this path and possibly spare him any future disappointments.

Tshepo was devastated by the decision but there was nothing he could do about it.

He became withdrawn and more isolated. I didn't know how to reach out to him. I figured he just needed some space. But something was different. Before, he could be moody, but he would snap out of it in a matter of hours and we would be friends again. Now he was sunk in his distant mood all the time. He hardly spoke. Actually, I think he stopped speaking altogether and I just didn't realise it.

It was difficult for me to make sense of what was going on and it took me a long time to understand that by this time I had in fact lost my first true friend in life, my hero. The dark hole of depression had swallowed him, but I didn't know it yet.

While most families in our township went all out to celebrate their children's 16th and 21st birthdays, our tradition was to wait until after confirmation for the party. It was our rite of passage. But when Tshepo finally got confirmed he chose a big Telefunken colour TV over a big, once-off party. Another boy, Tsilane, who lived just up the road and was confirmed at the same church, chose the party and he got presents on top of that. I think maybe Tshepo was just not up to having lots of people around for the celebration.

When it became clear that Tshepo was not really coping at school, my parents decided that perhaps a boarding school was a good idea. They hoped it would take him away from the negative influences in the streets near our home and in Alra Park. Westbury High School, which had a boarding facility, was one of the options. I don't actually know why, given the rough reputation that the area had. For me, Tshepo going from Alra Park to Westbury High seemed like going from bad to worse.

But on 10 December 1992, a week after schools had closed, we went as a family to Westbury High School so Tshepo could write his entrance test. We waited in the car while he wrote it. When he came back he was indifferent. The school told my parents that they would let them know the results.

After that we drove to Booysens, where the police kept stolen cars. Some months earlier my parents' first car, a cream-white Toyota Corolla 1.3, had been stolen at gunpoint in our yard just as my father was pulling into the gate. Now the police had found the car, and we were there to check it out. We saw that the car had been stripped of its insides, and the tyres and the radio were gone, but the shell of the vehicle was, surprisingly, still in good condition. My parents made arrangements with the police to have the car delivered closer to Springs and then we drove back home.

When we got there, Tshepo's school report for the year was in the pile of mail. He had dismally failed his Standard Six. My father left, to attend to some business. Tshepo and I prepared ourselves brown bread and eggs in the kitchen. When we sat down, my mother came in, flapping Tshepo's report in her hand, and she let loose. I'd never seen her this angry. She was shouting at the top of her voice, pacing up and down and banging her hand against the fridge and against the kitchen countertop.

She would fall quiet for a few moments, and then she would fire away again. It went on like that for about 40 minutes.

'*uDom na?* Are you dumb?'

'Is this what we send you to school for?'

TSHEPO

'What is this? What is this?'

'*Ke masepa fela a!* This is absolute shit!'

It was strange. It was usually my father who unleashed the fury but this time around it was my mother. I guess Tshepo's academic failure was a reflection on her and that's why she took it so personally. After a while she took herself off to her room.

We ate our lunch with our heads hung low. I felt sorry for Tshepo. Neither of us said a word.

Tshepo went to our room after he had finished eating, but after a few minutes he came back and made for the kitchen door. As he walked out he half turned towards me and he said, 'Bye'.

I nodded and carried on with my food.

He went to the garage to get something, and then he was gone. I thought perhaps he wanted to be alone to cool off.

When I had finished eating I went to the garage and grabbed my bicycle. I cycled around our neighbourhood looking for him, but he was nowhere. I thought that perhaps he had gone to Perm section to visit our cousins Kgotso and Bongane. I rode to their house, but he was not there. I lingered for a while and then I started back home again.

From afar, I saw *Malome* Butinyana's red Jetta and another car parked outside our house. *Good, some family visiting us for a change,* I thought. A feeling of excitement grew inside me as I cycled closer and closer to home. When I got there *Malome* Butinyana and some other guy were standing outside, having a cigarette.

I greeted them. They greeted me. Their demeanour was solemn. They told me to go inside. They were curt and I grew anxious.

When I walked in through the kitchen door there was a small party of people in the house, all of them looking glum, some neighbours and some family. There was this hushed kind of activity going on in the house that I couldn't put my finger on. Someone held me tightly and guided me to the living room. On the couch, my mother was sandwiched between both my grandmothers, and she was crying bitterly. Both my grandmothers were comforting her. My paternal grandmother asked me to take a seat. I settled comfortably next to her.

She held me close and with no hesitation she told me, '*Tshepo o ipolaile,* Tshepo has killed himself'.

That day physical and emotional pain became one. It was the worst agony I had ever felt. My heart was physically in pain and there was nothing I or anyone else could do to make it stop. In the morning I had woken up with Tshepo in the same room, and now, at night, I was to go back to the same room, all by myself, and he was never coming back. That thought played over and over in my head.

Tears flowed down my face deep into the night as I cried myself to sleep. I didn't sleep much.

The following day I woke up weak, and I cried again when I realised that it wasn't some bad dream. The nightmare was real. I would never see Tshepo again.

Over the next few days, as the funeral was being arranged, I learnt that after Tshepo had said 'Bye' to me at the kitchen door he had gone to the garage to get a rope. He had then walked a long distance, by his lonesome, to a piece of veld close to the Corobrik plant and Selcourt Extension 3. When he got there, he found a piece of cardboard, wrote our home address on it and then hanged himself from one of the trees. The rope snapped his neck and he soiled himself as he dangled lifelessly on that tree. A passer-by found him and then he or she called the police. The police came and loaded his body on the back of their van, and they brought him to our house, still with the rope around his neck and with his mouth agape, to verify if indeed he belonged to the address he had written down on that piece of cardboard. My mother was alone at the house and she had to identify his body.

As more family and friends arrived to offer their condolences, anger slowly grew inside me. Even though I was sad and shattered I became resentful about what Tshepo had done to me and to the family. Why couldn't he have been a little bit stronger mentally and emotionally? Why did he give up? Why did he not think about me? Why was he so selfish? And why did he choose such a horrible and painful way of dying?

Our family church, the Evangelical Lutheran Church, told my folks that they didn't normally officiate at the funeral services of people who had taken their own lives, but, since Tshepo had been a child of the church and had been confirmed in the church, they would make an exception. This was a good thing, I suppose, because I just couldn't see Tshepo's funeral service happening in our garage. He was well loved by his family and peers.

Then the Setswana saying '*Moipolai ga a lelelwe* – We don't cry over the ones who have taken their own lives,' started materialising in my spirit. Strangely enough, the idiom gave me some comfort and I told my cousins that I was done with crying over Tshepo. They said that I was lying to myself. They said that come the day of the funeral I would be the one crying the loudest.

The day of the funeral came, and I shed no tears. From photographs of that day I know I wore a dejected scowl on my face. When we went to the parlour to see his body for the last time, he was lying inside his casket, embalmed. He was wearing the grey suit that he had worn for his confirmation ceremony. His eyes were shut tight and sunken, and he had a neck brace on to keep his mouth closed. His mouth could no longer close on its own because of the way the rope had snapped his neck.

I was amongst the first to see him, and when I did I just leaned over his casket and said 'Bye,' just as he had said 'Bye' to me at the threshold of our kitchen door as he walked out a week earlier, and then I walked away. At the church service people were crying, many hysterically. My mother couldn't stop crying as speaker after speaker went up on stage to celebrate Tshepo's memory. A

A FATHER IS BORN

15-year-old boy had taken his own life after failing Standard 6. Many of Tshepo's peers were there, and I could see they were devastated. But still I shed no tears.

As his coffin slowly descended into the ground, rain clouds gathered and the sky darkened. My mother let out a wail so defeated that I wished I could take her pain away. At that moment I wished that I could bring Tshepo back from the dead, for her sake even more than mine. Trickles of rain started to fall as the men began moving the earth back into the ground with their shovels.

We made for the cars. It was all over. But still I shed no tears.

Of all the scars that I have had to live with, losing Tshepo is undoubtedly the worst. He was a teenager, a troubled soul who was also suffering terribly with his schooling. But the torment, psychological and physical, and the unrelenting pressure for him to do well at school persisted until he ended up taking his own life.

Tshepo means 'to have hope' or 'to have trust in the Lord'. My hope or my trust in the Lord died at that time in my life.

PART 3

8

Picking up the pieces
Part 1

A FATHER IS BORN

Losing Tshepo taught me that it is not by our own might or intelligence, but by grace, that we have life to begin with. It taught me that while grace is still upon us, then we owe it to life to live it, whether we like it or not. It taught me that life is such a great and powerful force because no matter how desperate your situation is, you still have to live it, you still have to wake up and try again, you still have to hope and to strive for a better tomorrow. Some people may argue that moving on and picking up the pieces is actually the cruellest part about life, and maybe there is some truth in that. But what choice do you have? For live you must, and live we did.

In January of 1993 we moved to the suburbs, to a quiet place called Sharon Park in Nigel. They say moving house is the second most traumatic experience a person can ever go through. The first one is losing someone close to you. I welcomed this so-called 'second most traumatic experience' with open arms. The move actually brought me comfort, because I did not want to be in Kwa-Thema any more. I no longer wanted to live in our old house, a house that had brought me so much pain and anguish. I no longer wanted to be in the same neighbourhood, around the people who knew what had happened, the same people who would forever feel sorry for me when they saw me. I felt that in their eyes. I had now become this 'poor kid whose brother hanged himself'. I didn't need any more stares piling on the misery.

We moved to a big house with an even bigger yard – one that both Tshepo and I had chosen while we were house-hunting with our parents the previous year. Family and close friends came over regularly to lighten up our lives. For a while there was some sunshine in my life, some veneer of hope. But I was no longer a child. I had seen and experienced too much.

My parents tried to make sure that our conversations were no longer top-down, but inclusive, from basic things like 'What would you like to have for supper?' or 'What kind of takkies would you like?' to deeper things like 'What would you like to be one day?' or 'What type of a house do you see yourself living in someday?' I was allowed to listen to whatever music I wanted to in my room, which was mostly rap music, and on weekends I was also allowed to stay up late to watch movies or popular music shows at the time, like *Zero Hour Zone* and *Toyota Top 20*.

It was clear that they were now approaching their parenting a little differently. I was encouraged to talk more, to come out of my shell more and to stop wallowing in self-pity so much. In fact, the only time they ever got upset with me was when I was feeling sorry for myself. My father, who was not a very expressive person, reached out to me by taking me to soccer games every other weekend. Together we'd go to places like Odi Stadium in Mabopane, PAM Brink Stadium in Springs and Ellis Park and FNB Stadium in Johannesburg to watch teams like Orlando Pirates, Moroka Swallows and Mamelodi Sundowns and our national team Bafana Bafana take on their rivals.

These excursions were the only time that I would see some life in his eyes, especially when he spoke about soccer. He would speak fondly about players from yesteryear, like Jomo Sono and 'Malombo' Lechaba. He was convinced that if it hadn't been for apartheid sports sanctions, those players could've won the soccer World Cup. His words rang true three years later in 1996, when our national team Bafana Bafana did indeed win the Africa Cup of Nations tournament, soon after being allowed to participate in international sport.

But my father was still this shadowy figure in my eyes. I still feared him, even though he was trying to show me a different side. I was always cautious around him, always making sure that I don't put a foot wrong.

On weekdays, I would often spend time in the afternoons with my mother, helping her in the garden. We talked a lot about what had happened. I knew that she was broken inside, even though she seemed to be fine on the outside. She asked me questions about how I felt. I answered as freely as I could. These afternoon gardening sessions were like therapy for both of us. We grew closer. Around March she fell pregnant again, and I couldn't wait to welcome my new brother or sister into the family.

———

One day, a few months after we had moved into the new house, we went to see a sangoma in the Barcelona informal settlement, close to the Vlakfontein mining area. I was confused, because we were a Christian family. I did not understand this visit that a family member or friend had suggested to my folks. I had never been to a sangoma before, let alone been inside a shack. I did not know what to expect. It was blistering hot in the shack and I sweated all the time. There were no proper tables or chairs, and we sat on straw mats. My parents consulted with the sangoma while I listened quietly. After the conversation, the sangoma prepared a blackened paste-like mixture inside an empty shoe polish can. He took a needle and dipped it in the mixture, then asked my parents to bring me closer. He pricked my forehead with this needle a number of times, while muttering some words. He gave me something to chew on and to spit out. I did as I was told.

After that I was instructed to wait outside in the car while the sangoma turned his attention to my parents. They came out about 30 minutes later. On our way home, I asked my mother what the visit was all about. She told me that it was to protect me, so that what had happened to Tshepo would not happen to me.

In my mind, I had now become this thing that had to be taken to sangomas for protection or to the graveyards for blessings and for good luck. I had now become this thing that needed to be cleansed. I grew to really hate myself and my life after that. I truly wished that I was somebody else.

———

On 1 November 1993, a day before my mother was scheduled for her first and only caesarean operation, she asked me what she should name the baby. I was caught off guard by the question. I had been looking forward to the arrival of the new baby into the family. During the pregnancy I used to marvel at the small bumps that would pop up when the baby kicked my mother's stomach. Sometimes she would let me put my hand on her stomach so I could feel the kicks.

I was going to be the big brother now and my mother was asking me what she should name the baby. I could see that she was serious.

'Tumelo,' I said.

'OK,' she responded with a smile. I liked the name because it closely resembled my own name, and also because it was the name of my best friend Neo's little brother. About two days later, my mother came back home from the hospital with a new baby boy called Tumelo. I was proud of myself for having named him. I had grown up thinking that only parents or grandparents could name people. But now there I was, a proud new member of the christening club. I felt like my voice was actually being heard, like I was an integral part of the family unit and not just a member.

There was an 11-year gap between Tumelo and me, and I knew that we could never be as close as I had been with Tshepo, but I was still thankful to have a baby brother. Tumelo brought light into my life. He had big eyes and big cheeks and the most wonderful smile I had ever seen. I loved him and I was protective over him. I took him everywhere with me. He had such a gentle and calm soul. I knew that my parents had him just for me. Otherwise, they would not have bothered to have another baby, because things were really not good between the two of them, even though they pretended they were.

One day I went to my cousin Bongane's house for a weekend

visit. When I came back home that Sunday evening I found Tumelo walking. But it was really more like he was running from couch to couch. I was moved by how quickly he was growing and how independent he was becoming. In no time he was also talking. He had excellent vocabulary and perfect sentence construction. For a while, as I watched him growing up, I forgot my pain.

After Tumelo was born my parents' fights grew more frequent. I don't know if they were secretly blaming each other for what had happened, but their love for each other seemed to have vanished. My mother went back to teaching at night school, for some extra cash. She stopped going to church and eventually we stopped going to church as a family altogether. My father started spending more time away from home, either at the sports stadiums watching soccer games, or at the Home Sweepers' Society Club – a *stokvel* that he was a part of – with his buddies. He started dressing smartly again, dousing himself with Old Spice whenever he went out.

My mother was no fool. She suspected that he was probably having an affair, as he had in the past. She knew not only about the Hebron one, but about another, with a certain Mistress Mokoena, the same Mistress Mokoena who had assisted me with my name situation back in Sub A (Grade 1). At primary school we referred to teachers as Mistress so-and-so and Meneer so-and-so. It was only later that I learnt that it was actually inappropriate to refer to a female teacher as a 'mistress'. The appropriate term to use was Madam, Ma'am or Mam'. But back then, Mistress Mokoena was really a mistress, both as a teacher and in terms of her extramarital status. The affair happened when I was in Standard 1, though of course I knew nothing about it at the time. My mother's older sister, Aunty Dolly, who taught the Sub Bs (Grade 2s) at the school had suspected that something was happening between those two. One day, she had found a crumpled-up note which read 'I love you' that my father had thrown into the staffroom bin during break time. Aunty Dolly had put two and two together and deduced that the letter could only have been from Mam' Mokoena. She told my mother, and then things quickly got uncomfortable for my father at the school. Given the history, I would say that my mother was within her rights to be suspicious.

She started drinking alcohol and gambling at casinos like the Morula Sun in Mabopane and the Carousel close to Warmbaths, now Bela-Bela, just outside of Pretoria. In no time she became a functional gambling addict. Functional in the sense that she would be with us in the early evening, cooking supper and seeing to it that my schoolwork was done, and then once we went to bed she would drive to her casinos of choice and only come back in the early hours of the morning. We were definitely under some financial strain, especially with our new suburban lifestyle of shopping malls, takeaways and Model C schools. But I think that the gambling was her way of getting away, of escaping her life for just a couple of hours, just as my father probably did, secretly, in the arms of another woman.

It was around this time, 1995, that my mother also got herself involved with a popular pyramid scheme called Gold Dust. She threw her all into it. She would spend many nights away from home recruiting new members into the scheme. She was always on the go. I suppose it was her way of coping with things. I think she knew that maybe if she stopped to think, or to just be, then she would fall apart, so being busy was her way of keeping herself together. At first the pyramid scheme money was coming in thick and fast and she was convinced that she was on her way to riches.

My father was not convinced at all and he wanted no part of it. In the same year he was appointed as the new principal of Sechaba Primary School, taking over from Meneer Sekgapane, and he probably felt that it was unbecoming for an 'upstanding' headmaster to be embroiled in such a scheme. He would get really annoyed with the different people coming in and out of the house, people that my mother was trying to recruit. He would be even more irritated when, for security reasons, he had to drive my mother around to deliver money to the members whose pay day had come.

But in less than six months Gold Dust came crashing down. One afternoon when I was home alone there was a telephone call. At the other end was the voice of an unfriendly and threatening male.

'Is your mother at home?' he asked.

'No, sorry,' I said.

'Tell her to watch her back,' warned the voice, before hanging up.

It was a clear death threat. I was scared, but I didn't want to panic. I thought of calling the police. But I also thought that perhaps by calling the police I would be making the situation worse. This was a time before cellphones, so I also couldn't immediately warn her. I was relieved when I heard her car pull up in the driveway in the early evening.

When she heard about the call she told me that 'It's just these crazy Gold Dust people' and she said that she didn't know why they wanted money from her. She told me not to worry about it. 'It's nothing, I promise you,' she said.

But I could feel that something serious was brewing with this Gold Dust situation. One night I heard a hushed but very intense discussion between her and my father in their room. A couple of weeks later, she came home in the afternoon with her face swollen up and bruised on one side. There were deep cuts in her flesh. When I asked her about it, she said she had fallen and that it was nothing. But I knew that it had something to do with 'these crazy Gold Dust people'.

PICKING UP THE PIECES PART 1

My father was not at all impressed with how things were unravelling around this pyramid scheme or with the fact that he was indirectly involved with it through my mother. I don't know how, but my mother did eventually manage to get herself out of the pyramid scheme, and there was no more talk of Gold Dust around the house.

I, on the other hand, was evolving into a somewhat indifferent teenager who wallowed in self-pity and a lack of confidence. In Grade 8 I started at an all-boys' school, Springs Boys' High. One day, two boys in my class, Morgan and Kgaugelo, started asking me questions about Tshepo and how he died. I could tell that they already knew and they were asking merely to see how I would react. The kids at the school who knew me from my old neighbourhood knew exactly what happened and they had the decency not to bring up the subject, at least not in my presence.

I didn't give them the satisfaction of seeing me break down and cry. I just told them that I didn't know what had happened to my brother. I told them that he was probably shot or something. I told them that my parents had never really told me what happened. But honestly, I was too ashamed to tell them that he had hanged himself. I had not made peace with that. It still hurt. For the rest of my classes that day I was numb. After school I went straight home.

My parents had not given me the keys to the main house yet, so for now I had to use the back room, behind the garage, until they came back from work. I went to the back room. And I broke down. I cried for what felt like hours. I could not stop crying. I was angry with those boys for asking me those questions. I was angry that my big brother was not around any more to defend me. I was angry at him that he had taken his own life and left me all alone to face this God-forsaken world.

I cried until my head felt heavy and I had no more tears to cry.

A FATHER IS BORN

I sat there deep in thought, meditating on my pain and the humiliation I had hidden in class.

My mind ached with thoughts. *Why was I born? Nobody asked me if I wanted to be born. Why the hell do we live? Why did my brother have to die? Who holds all the answers? Don't tell me it's God. Who is God? I don't know God. Who is he really? A spirit? A supernatural being with all the answers? Some say God is abstract, a miracle felt, not seen. Well, God must be choosy then, because I've never felt nor seen any miracles.*

Tshepo had been my source of comfort when I came home with a black eye. He was my alibi when trouble was near, and in times of danger he would always appear. I used to follow him everywhere, like a Rottweiler next to its master, ready to attack anybody who tried to mess up our name. Now I was left to roam all alone. After this, writing in my scrapbook became an outlet for me. I even had a diary, which I ended up burning, afraid that someone might find it and then get to read what really went on in my mind and heart, things not spoken, but that lived voluminously in my psyche.

My present is a dying future and a past that just lives on and on. I close in with dusk and I wake a soiled soul with dawn. I'm a seed dispersed in the wastelands and I grow as a weed. Despair is the ground I stand upon. The days are the same. Through ashes of burnt-out letters I hear my name. Involuntarily my heart starts hoping. Tell me it ain't so. Tell me it ain't so. No, you are lying. It can't be true. But it is.

When your head aches there's an aspirin. But when your heart aches you are left searching. Defeated and stranded. Confused and alone. Eyes bloodshot and swollen from all the crying, so that you can't even see the clear blue skies that God is trying to show you. Everything is dark and diseased.

From seed, child to man, curse-driven is your lifespan. You go insane from drowning in this endless rain of pain. You constantly feel like you've reached your depths. Worn-out like you've been running endless laps. Every day is another relapse, another misstep. Your life is one big mishap. You have no rest, no peace.

On bended knees next to your bed your heart bleeds. The devil deceives. Your soul he receives. In search of peace you climb the highest peak. But still of death you reek. Your heart screams of broken dreams, dreams hung and left to gasp for scraps like stray dogs nosing around a heap of rubbish, and solemnly you wonder whether to pray for a new breath or for a quick death.

Your soul, a landscape of barren lands, cloudless skies, empty horizons, dry vegetation thirsting for a drop of rain and scorching heat ripples refracting from the ground up. A soul constantly haunted by the ghostly silence of your surrounds and the noisy horror of your thoughts that keep replaying, over and over again, your failures and disappointments.

So you go through life searching for backdoors to take the exit. Mr One-Man, solo with no team. It's the diaries of high school with corridors filled with peers with no feelings, shooting nasty remarks like bullets. So you dwell in Rhythm and Poetry for some solace and insight.

'Raw rapping, records rotating, radical realism, refuting righteous reasoning, raising rampant riots, racketing rattles and raging rhythms'.

You wish to burn your scrapbook notes so that your words can travel in fumes and clog the brains of many so they can know how you feel. Your narration laments upon your longing to unleash the beast of words so you can one day free the enslaved YOU.

My pain, written in scarlet ink across double-margined pages, documented in similes, metaphors ... now ages. I'm a dying man with a pen and a pad, a slave to my mistress' jealousy, seduced by her innocence and her promise of freedom, choked by her words that are constantly suffocating my wild-spirited heart/art that now finds itself defeated in dramatic irony.

My mind is a concentration camp. Congested. Caged. Cemented in chaos. I'm scared to even look in the mirror because mirrors tell reflections and mine is a broken one, broken into pieces with sharp edges.

I just want to go home. I want to go home. I want to go home. I just want to die so I can live forever in spirit. I want to shed so my wandering happiness can amend once again. I want to go home. But where is home? I don't know but it can't possibly be this hell that I'm currently living in right now, where a cold and a violent storm is my perpetual season.

But then one day my older self, from the future, decides to pay me a visit. He whispers redemption in my ears. He speaks of the reconstruction of ruins. He speaks of restoration, a rekindling of lost relationships. He speaks of reconciliation. He tells me it's time to rejoice, time to remove remorse from my life, time for rehabilitation. He speaks of a revolutionary remedy within that will bring rejuvenation, reformation, and renewal.

'I know it's hard for you to trust anyone, right, but I'm here for you, I'm here for us,' he tells me.

'In time your heart will heal and together we can amend these scars, your scars, our scars,' he tells me. 'Then we can both escape this life together. We were both born into this life. We live it. We've lived it. Like you I'm a dreamer and I know that you have forgotten how to dream.'

'But I'm here to remind you how to dream once again,' he tells me.

'I see beyond your current pain,' he tells me. 'Beyond your hopeless surrounds ... beyond the chilly lonely nights and beyond the sad long days ... I see beyond the evil smoke that blurs stars from the skies. I'm a dreamer. I close my eyes and see visions of a better tomorrow.'

'I know that you have been writing,' he tells me, '... scribbling your pain page after page and I know that the pain is still there no matter what you do. But I need you to stop writing and to start re-writing,' he tells me. 'Re-write your life, your destiny, our destiny.'

'Rise!' he orders me. 'Levitate like spaceships. Be lethal like snake pits. Rise above so you can see through all these lies that disguise stars in the dark skies.'

I look at him and I ask him of the possibilities of being... the possibilities of being able to just watch the moon and the stars outside without being labelled soft and weak. I ask him of the possibilities of feeling good when I'm feeling sad. I ask him of the possibilities of listening to my music with the volume up, all day long without a care in the world. I ask him of the possibilities of laughing out loud and endlessly as if I were a kid again. I ask him of the possibilities of wandering about freely through my life.

I ask him of the possibilities of finally being free from this world's outrageous demands. Of the possibilities of meditation? Of enlightenment? Of reaching a higher plateau in this journey of self? Of forgiveness? Of forgetting? And of not forgetting to forgive? Of living? Of escaping this world? Of escaping this life? Of escaping myself? Of escaping my mind? And of escaping of my heart?

He tells me, 'Yes it's all possible, and much more...'

Then I dream of the angels of darkness chasing me. Their faces are painted with blood. As they close in on me I trip and I fall. These angels of darkness grab me and take me with them to the underworld. Light disappears and darkness takes over. But I can still see clearly. This underworld is cold, trees are dying out and everyone is wearing black.

They lead me on the path they say I'm destined to walk. I see my brother Tshepo. But it's not really him. It looks just like my brother but in my spirit I know that it's not him. I don't know who this person is. I don't feel anything. Nothing moves me inside. The figure or ghost or spirit is of his likeness but it's not really him.

A FATHER IS BORN

It dawns on me that Tshepo is gone, that he has been gone for a while, and I just didn't realise it. I was just hanging on to the memories of old. The brother that I know had actually left me a long time ago. He had left me even when he was still alive, and that which is reflected before me is not my reality.

When I wake in the morning I talk with my older future self again. He's not around any more but I talk to him anyhow. I know he's listening. I tell him that I want to run away with him because he is all that I have. I tell him that I have thought extensively about what he told me, about seeing beyond and escaping to better days. I tell him that while I was sitting in my room, all by myself, listening closely to my thoughts, trying to figure out what might have gone wrong, I thought that no fairytale or fantasy in the world could compare to the blissful and eternal love that he has for me and I for him, and staying in a space that was constantly clipping my wings whenever I was preparing to fly was just not beneficial for both of us. So that's why I have to leave, I tell him. That's why I'm choosing him. That's why I want to run away with him. You are really all that I have, self, I tell him. I have no choice but to be much kinder to you, to us, I tell him.

9

Life lessons

A FATHER IS BORN

Some people believe that life is one big lesson that we are all supposed to learn from. For those who subscribe to this particular school of thought, the lesson, rather than the physical, breathing manifestation part of life, is actually the gift. It is believed that some people are quick studies while others need a lifetime or two to learn even one lesson – but learn we all must. But I wonder if the lesson is intended to help us in this lifetime or in another. And I wonder if the life experience is really worth the lesson.

Was the traumatic experience of losing Tshepo really worth the lesson – whatever that lesson was? Was there no other way we could've learnt the lesson, maybe? And what becomes of the lesson itself if the experience completely changes who you are?

We all had to move on with our lives after Tshepo, as broken as we were. We all had to pick up the pieces and try to salvage whatever we could of our lives. We had no choice but to embrace a new life without pondering the 'why' all the time, for if we did that, I believe, we would've been defeated for sure.

While my parents were trying their best to not be as they were before, I was wrestling with just being.

One day, when I was in Grade 9, our history teacher instructed us to draw a tree. I was a pretty good artist, and I drew a tree that resembled the many trees I had seen on the covers of fairytale books in my childhood. She walked from desk to desk looking at our trees. When she got to my drawing, she commented that the broken branches I had drawn symbolised that I had been through a very traumatic experience in my family. She was right about the traumatic experience in my family bit, but I was really just going for a realistic tree, and hoping that she would be impressed by my artistic take on it. I didn't know it was some psycho-analytical experiment. She moved on to my friend Zee, who had drawn a tree full of blooms, with lots of fruits hanging from it. She commented that Zee's drawing meant that he was happy and that he came from a loving family. *But Zee has also lost an older brother, in a tragic car accident, and he also doesn't get along with his father,* I thought. I was quite baffled, actually angered, by this class assessment. It would annoy me for years to come. I felt that she really didn't know me but still felt it necessary to 'label' me in that class based on some drawing. I grew indifferent towards teachers after that. My schoolwork showed it. But I didn't care and that became a shield for me. Not caring.

Briefly, in 1997, when I was in Grade 10, I began to come into my own again. I started noticing girls and playing basketball. I wrote a poem about myself at the time.

> *A black boy is what my features define.*
> *My complexion is earthy, others prefer to say ebony.*
> *I have a heart-shaped face and a high forehead.*
> *My eyes are nothing special, just a black dot in the middle of a white surrounding.*
> *My nose is broad and sturdy, with nostrils like caves.*
> *I have a long scar tearing across my right cheek from childhood, prominently exhibited for the whole world to see.*
> *My lips are thick and full: some prefer to call them Dunlop tyres.*
> *My teeth are healthy, but they are long and they stick out every time I smile.*
> *My hair is not straight, but fluffy and puffy from the constant exploitation of western hair chemicals.*
> *I'm well-built but like a hunger-stricken child my ribs stick out like horns.*
> *But I am beautiful.*

I found myself giving Christianity a second try that same year. One day I was invited to a church called His People by the daughter of the pastor. The church services were held in a classroom at the Thembalikazulu Primary School in Kwa-Thema. It was not what I was accustomed to, but I gave it a chance. The atmosphere was warm and friendly and the services were small and intimate, more like a family gathering than formal church. The praising and worshipping were uninhibited. I especially liked how just anybody could walk up to the front of the church and share their testimonies. I kept going back, and I even joined the Student Christian Association at school. I stopped listening to the likes of Snoop Dogg and listened more to Kirk Franklin. But one day my father walked into the living room and found me with my head buried deep in the Bible. With a perturbed look, he told me to ease up on this born-again Christian stuff.

'You are just burdening yourself right now with all this religion,' he told me. 'Just relax and enjoy life.'

So I stopped. I don't know why he felt it necessary to dissuade me, but just like that, I was back to factory settings. The downward spiral of self-loathing and of not caring flowed into the new year. Twice I made it to the principal's office. The first time I was sent to Mr French's office was for being disruptive in class. Our biology teacher, Mrs Holland, had accused me of talking during her lessons and of shouting 'Black Power', which I absolutely do not recall. Though maybe I did raise a Black Power fist as she was kicking me out of her class. The second time was for not applying myself to my schoolwork generally. My schoolbooks were always in tatters and they were always mixed up. One would find Afrikaans and biology notes in the same book, for example.

On both occasions my parents were called in and on both occasions my father let it slide. He had no choice, because the kind of trouble I was in needed to be corrected by more than just a smacking. A no-nonsense judo enthusiast, Mr French told my parents straight that I was in danger of failing my Grade 11 come the end of the year.

'If he doesn't pull up his socks then I'm afraid you will have to find him another school, because Springs Boys' High is simply no place for such a learner,' he said firmly to my parents.

My father, a principal himself, just sat there and listened quietly like some schoolboy.

It had been years since my father last laid hands on me. In fact, he no longer subscribed to the idea of physical punishment as a means of straightening out a child. Before, all he knew was to lash out in anger to get his point across. But now he was controlling himself. He was watching his outbursts. He was checking the instinctual violence that he used to unleash at the slightest of irritations. I don't know if Tshepo's death had broken him or if it had made him better, but I think there was just no going back for him and he was not prepared to lose yet another son. Instead, he preferred us to talk whenever there was an issue and I was not playing ball. I was passive-aggressive actually, because during these talks I would just sit on the couch in the living room, quietly, while he spoke, and I would get up and go back to my room when he was finished.

None of these interventions by adults did much to improve my school performance or my general outlook on life. I became more despondent and gloomy. The only subject that I cared about was English. I still kept my diary for my pain and I had a scrapbook for my rhymes. I looked out for metaphors and similes in books like George Orwell's *Animal Farm,* John Steinbeck's *Of Mice and Men* and Harper Lee's *To Kill a Mockingbird*. I was intrigued by the dichotomous nature of people like Macbeth and Brutus in the plays by William Shakespeare. To this day I still ponder all of humanity in that light, not as one-dimensional but as eternally flawed and multi-layered. I enjoyed watching and breaking down films like Baz Luhrmann's *Strictly Ballroom* and *Romeo + Juliet* as part of the film study lessons that we did in the English course. I loved stories. But more than anything I wanted to tell my own stories. Maybe it was my way of trying to articulate the emotional turmoil that I was going through.

A FATHER IS BORN

That year I picked up the habit of smoking, I started experimenting with alcohol and I even spent a night away from home once.

One day, TKZee, the popular Kwaito group, was billed to perform at the Springs Indoor Sports Centre. Everyone was going to be there, and I could not miss it. So I lied to my parents. I told them that I was going to sleep over at my cousin Bongane's place. I knew that I was going to get caught out, because my mom and Bongane's mom, Aunty Dolly, spoke all of the time, but I just did not care. I had to be there. Come to think of it now, I was not even a fan of TKZee and there was no 'special girl' that I was supposed to meet there. But peer pressure got the better of me. I don't know if TKZee had cancelled, or if they were just running late, but when I arrived no one seemed to care because the partying was going on right there, outside the Springs Indoor Sports Centre. There was drinking of alcohol, music blaring from every second car or taxi, boys mixing with girls and girls mixing with boys. It was an all-out bash, right there, just next to the Springs Town Council buildings.

The Metro police had their hands full that night. I had been there before with my parents for some wrestling event and when the Boswell Wilkie Circus was in town. But I had never seen the place turned upside down like that. I hooked up with some friends of mine, and I used the money that I had for the entrance fee to chip in so we could all buy ourselves some beer. 'One man, one *ngudu*,' was our favourite saying back then, which simply meant that each man gets his own quart of beer to drink. I was not much of a drinker, so that one quart probably lasted me the whole night. We partied outside the Springs Indoor Sports Centre until the sun came up, literally. We then walked to the rank to catch a taxi home.

I slept for most of the day. I felt like I had flown too close to the sun this time around and I was mentally ready for any kind of punishment. But my parents did nothing. My mother gave me a long speech about the dangers of AIDS and of drug use. I was not engaging in sexual activity nor was I taking drugs, but she could still see that I was definitely on a self-destructive path.

———

At the time I also felt that if I could change schools then my life would improve. I was fed up with this all-boys school and I felt that if I could move to a co-ed environment then things would be better for me. I don't know why I felt so strongly that this was what I really needed.

'Why do you want to change schools?' asked my mother when I brought up the subject one night after supper. There was the bullying, the subtle racism, the authoritarian style of leadership, the domineering white institutional culture or even the general stealing of student belongings that went on at the school that I was now sick and tired of, but I just couldn't give her a convincing answer.

'I want to play soccer and there's no soccer at Boys',' I answered. Out of the corner of my eye, I could see my father try to suppress a chuckle that was desperately trying to escape. It was no secret that I was more successful at basketball than I was at soccer.

My mother humoured me. 'So, what school do you have in mind?'

The only school I could think of was Nigel High School.

'Nigel High is far away and the kids there are not disciplined,' she said.

Veritas College was probably my next option. But it was a private school and there was no way my parents were going to pay those school fees.

'We are not taking you out of Boys', my baby. I like Mr French. He is a good principal,' she said.

A FATHER IS BORN

I scowled with a lump in my throat and I kept my eyes trained on the floor as I usually did when I couldn't get my way.

'What are you running away from?' asked my father, amused.

'I'm not running away from anything. I just don't like Boys' any more,' I said.

'You are running away from something,' he pressed.

'I'm not,' I insisted.

'In life we must face our challenges head on. Every place has its own challenges. Running away doesn't help to solve any problems,' he said.

'And it would be very irresponsible of us to let you change schools during this time of the year,' said my mother. 'You are staying at Boys' and you are going to make it work. You can't run away from situations all the time. If you don't want Boys' then you can go to Nkumbulo or Phulong back in Kwa-Thema,' she chided.

The following morning, as my father was driving me to school, without my mother present, I took my chance again. 'I really don't want to go Boys' any more,' I said.

My father said nothing. He just kept on driving. When we arrived at school I climbed out of his car, grabbed my school bag and told him that I was not going to school. I don't know where I got the courage to pull such a stunt. It was so out of character – I suppose it was indicative of the emotional state I was in. I was angry at life and at that moment my anger overpowered any fear that I had of my father. My posture was defiant, almost as if I were daring him, proving that he could do whatever he wanted to do, but I was still not going to school that day.

With my school bag hanging over one shoulder I began making my way back home on foot. As I walked I heard the morning bell ring, summoning the learners to assembly, but I just kept on walking, homebound. My father turned his car around and he followed behind me slowly for a while. Then he pulled up next to me. He rolled down his window and told me to jump in.

'I'll drop you at home,' he said.

'But aren't you going to be late for work?' I asked.

'It's fine,' he assured me.

I climbed back in the car. Along the way he pulled over to the side of the road and switched off the engine.

What's wrong?' he asked.

'I don't want to go to Boys' any more,' I said.

'But why?' he asked.

'I just don't want to any more,' I said.

I don't think I even knew why. All I knew was that I wanted to go to a different school. That was all. We sat quietly in the car for about ten minutes. Both of us engaged in our own thoughts, oblivious of our surroundings and of the time.

'It's the middle of the year, Tumiso. Your mother and I cannot let you change schools, unfortunately. It's just way too late now. Plus Boys' is a good school,' he said, obviously having given it some thought.

Without saying a word, I got out of the car and began walking again. My father started the engine and drove behind me for a while before he pulled up alongside me again and asked me to please come back inside.

I complied. There were some cars passing by and I guess I was mindful not to make a scene.

He could tell that I was highly emotional and he was not prepared to leave me alone, even if it meant him being late for work. Once I was inside the car we sat there quietly for what felt like hours to me. I even cried at some point. He held me close. He told me that he loved me and that he cared about me very much. My head felt heavy afterwards and my body was weak.

When we arrived home, he told me to just sleep for the rest of the day. I think I slept in my school uniform. By the afternoon I was feeling a lot better and I had made peace with the fact that I was definitely going to be spending the remainder of my schooling years at Boys' whether I liked it or not.

It would take me years to realise that me wanting to change schools had nothing to do with Boys', but had everything to do with me wanting to get away from everything which had become familiar. I was scared of becoming too familiar with any one thing, because my experience was that familiarity does indeed breed contempt. My heart had already been broken once by someone with whom I was very familiar.

I think my desire to change schools was really more about staying detached, because when you are detached from places, institutions, people or things then nothing and no one can really hurt you. Losing someone so dear to me very early on in life changed how I felt about anything that represented stability, consistency and security.

It is still true. At face value I may seem to conform to popular societal norms of familial relations, of companionship, of attachment, of closeness and so on, but deep down I'm a very detached person who rarely allows people in. Anything long-term soon disappoints and that's why a big part of me always wants to stay detached from things, from people and from places. That way, there's less room for disappointment. I don't know if I've always been this type of a person or if it was the life experience that made me this way.

I also wonder what type of a person I would've turned out to be had my parents allowed me to change schools at that juncture. Would I have become a person who ups and leaves whenever situations are not going my way? Would I have been the type of person who has little appetite to fight difficult situations? Would I have turned out to be a happy person, someone with no baggage, who can leave people and things at the drop of a hat? I don't know. But staying definitely taught me how to be resilient and how to face any challenge that comes my way head on.

LIFE LESSONS

My father was certainly trying to be a better father this time around and I knew this, but a big part of me was just not giving him a chance. I was so trapped in my own feelings. It was six years since Tshepo had passed but I still blamed him for it, and I also blamed him for what had happened to me psychologically and emotionally since then. Subconsciously, I wanted him to suffer. I wanted to punish him by not meeting him halfway in his new quest to mend our relationship. But he *was* trying. I was now 16 years old, at a stage where going with him to watch soccer matches on weekends no longer held any appeal. So he reached out to me by giving me driving lessons. Most of the boys my age in our neighbourhood already knew how to drive, and I was more than keen to get behind the wheel.

My father had been the first in his family to learn how to drive. The only mode of transport his father Tshungwane ever propelled was a bicycle. So my father had no one to teach him how to drive and there was no car to speak of. But when he started to earn a decent salary in 1991 he took himself to a driving school and also bought himself his very first car, a cream-white Toyota Corolla 1.3. I don't know if it was an administrative error or what, but the car was, peculiarly, registered as a 'mini bus with the capacity to carry 14 black persons and their personal luggage' and it also came with a public permit that allowed my father to operate within the magisterial district of Springs. According to the papers, the vehicle was to be stationed at the taxi rank at the corner of Majola and Thema roads when not transporting people. But in reality, it was a family car, which always slept in our garage whenever it was not on the road.

On the first day of the lessons, he took me to an open soccer field in his red Toyota Corolla 1.6 GSE, popularly known as the 'Kentucky Rounder' in the townships, which he always kept in immaculate condition. His affinity for Toyota would be passed down to me some years down the line.

At the field we switched seats. The first thing he taught me was to make sure that the car was in neutral and that the handbrake was lifted up before starting the car. He took me through the basics, starting with the mirrors. He stressed that I should always use my indicators well before time, not just when I was already turning. He pointed to a button with a red triangle sign.

'This is the hazard light. Always remember to use this whenever you are having some trouble with the vehicle. It's to alert the other drivers that something is wrong,' he said.

I kept nodding enthusiastically. I wanted him to finish with the basics so I could start driving. 'The pedal on your right is the accelerator, the one in the middle is the brake and the one on your left is the clutch. The middle pedal is the most important one. Always use your brakes ...'

After what felt like hours, I was expecting to start driving soon. But how wrong I was. We stayed stationary while he carried on talking.

'Apply pressure on the clutch. Put the car in first gear. Release the hand brake. Gently release your foot off the clutch while applying pressure on the accelerator. Apply pressure on the clutch and gently release pressure on the accelerator ...'

He took me through all the gears like this, for a good 30 minutes. I felt like the Karate Kid being told by Mister Miyagi to 'wax on and wax off.'

It would take until the third lesson for me to move the car without it jolting to a dead stop. But as soon as I got the hang of it I had other problems to contend with, like learning how to apply less pressure on the accelerator. 'Stick to 20,' my father would remind me, exasperated. But I would have a lapse in concentration and find myself doing about 25 kilometers an hour as I drove around in circles on the field.

In about three months I could start and drive the car around in circles at 20 kilometers an hour and come to a perfect stop. I was raring to go. But like Mister Miyagi my father just kept on instructing me to do the same thing over and over again.

One weekend I was left at home alone while my parents went away to Sun City for a romantic rendezvous. But instead of looking after the house, I got into my father's car. I had still not ventured into third gear and fourth gear and I still did not know how to reverse. I could only go forward.

Luckily, our garage was built in such a way that the back opened up into the backyard. So instead of reversing I opened the gates, slowly drove forward into the yard, made a U-turn and then pulled out of the garage.

I drove out and left the gate open. I thought it would be easier for me when I came home because of how steep the driveway pavement was. I planned to go around the neighbourhood and maybe to the shops and then come back. I was cruising in first and second gear – I did not know then that I was actually killing the car by doing that. I was just happy to be behind the wheel and I was hoping that one of my friends would spot me.

Lo and behold, as I turned right into Napier Avenue, the suburb's outlying boundary road, a group of my friends, amongst them a girl that I kind of liked and that I would later take to my matric farewell, were walking to the shops.

My heart skipped a beat as I got closer and closer. I rolled my window all the way down and I slanted my seat just a little. As I sneaked up behind them, I hooted excitedly, and they scurried off to make way. When they saw that it was me, they were amazed. I popped my head out of the window, greeted them and carried on driving. From the rear-view mirror, I could see them hailing me to stop. But I didn't. I couldn't anyway. What if I stopped and the car jerked before coming to a dead stop? And what if I tried to start the engine again only to find that the car was still in gear and not in neutral? I could not risk the embarrassment. What they saw was good enough. Me behind the wheel, propelling the vehicle forward.

As I drove, alternating between first and second gear, a thought hit me. Why not quickly drive to Selcourt, the suburb just next to ours, and see what my cousin Bongane and his friends were up to? I used the back route to get to Selcourt, but there was no sign of Bongane and his friends and I decided to drive back home as it was getting dark. I used the safe back routes, cleverly, I thought.

But turning right into Rhokana from Molyneux is a bit tricky. There is a T-junction with a circle in the middle and no stop sign but a yield sign and a speed hump. I reduced my speed as I approached. I went over the hump with relative ease. I yielded. There was no oncoming traffic from either side.

Driving around the circle, my foot was just slightly on the brake pedal when it should have been all the way in, and the car was still moving fairly fast. I turned the steering wheel hard, but I still could not make a perfect turn. The left side of the bumper nicked the side of the pavement and the car wobbled as I struggled to get it back under control.

Thankfully, I did. I was now on Rhokana, a straight road with no sharp turns or bends, heading home. I could hear the left side of the bumper flapping against the car. When I arrived I pulled into the steep entrance with more or less the same degree of speed as I had done the circle bend, and this time, the right side of the bumper scraped against the side of the wall.

With the car now safely inside the yard I pulled over to have a proper look. The bumper was badly damaged. With both my hands on my head, I trembled with fear. How could I have driven so far with no major incident only to bugger up the car at home? But it was spilt milk. I would have to tell my parents that I had been messing around in the yard, I thought. I hopped back in the car. Started the engine. Put the car in gear.

As I was pulling in, I scraped the right side of the car against the steel frame of the garage. I stopped immediately. I had come in very awkwardly. I could not reverse or go forward. Whatever move I chose would do more damage to the vehicle. But I could not just leave it there either, halfway in and halfway out. So I put the car in first gear and I slowly drove forward, scraping the side, until I was finally through. I climbed out. I inspected the damage. It was bad.

I went inside for some water. I had no appetite at all. I kept replaying the events of the day in my head. How could I have been so stupid? All for what? To impress some friends in the streets. Now I was in the worst kind of trouble for sure. My father was going to kill me with his bare hands, I thought. I went back outside to do another inspection. I clipped the bumper back in place. It looked better. But it was still bruised and misaligned. I looked at the right side of the car. The big scratch stretched from the fender to the rear passenger door. It was a nightmare.

I went inside the house again. I poured hot water in a bucket and I mixed it with Handy Andy. I grabbed the bucket and a cloth, and I went outside to the garage. It was now dark. I cleaned the right side of the car for about an hour, trying to remove any surface marks. It looked a bit better, but the car was still dented, and the original red spray-paint job was flaking off.

So, genius me decided to get paint from the backroom. It was red matt paint that was meant only for house use. Then Picasso me grabbed a paintbrush. The light in the garage was not so good. I was relying heavily on the bathroom light coming from the house as I proceeded to cover up my tracks with gentle brushstrokes. A slight feeling of relief came over me as scratch marks disappeared with each brushstroke.

Satisfied with my cover-up work I retired inside for a hot bubble bath. I still had no appetite. I did manage to get some sleep,

A FATHER IS BORN

although barely. When my parents arrived back home it was past midnight. They locked up and went straight to bed.

By morning I was feeling a lot better. Mentally I had prepared myself. I was going to own up to my actions and I was going to face the consequences, however dire. My mother was busy sorting out the washing. My father was still sleeping. I crept slowly into the scullery.

'I have something to tell you,' I said to my mother. I did not tell her about the joy ride. 'I was just messing around in the yard. I really didn't mean for anything bad to happen,' I told her.

She was calm. She could see how worried and sorry I was. 'It is a good thing that you told me. Go to your room. I will talk with your father,' she said.

I stayed in my room for the whole day. I came out only when it was necessary and when I knew for sure that I would not cross my father's path.

My mother spoke to my father. When she came back to me she told me that all was well. I wanted to cry. But held back my tears.

'Your father is fine but very upset. I'd suggest that you stay out of his way for a while,' she advised.

When I inspected my paint job in clearer light it was messy and smudgy. The car now had an ugly two-tone shade of red. I should have just left it with the scratch marks and dents, I thought. That looked so much better in comparison with my cover-up work.

My father did not talk to me for weeks after that. Nothing. No shouting. No outburst. Nothing. It was the worst silent treatment I had ever endured.

'It's good that he is not talking because I don't know what he might do if he opened his mouth,' my mother told me.

Instead of continuing to engage me as he had started doing, he decided to disengage, to contain his rage, to be silent, and this angered me, ironically. I was feeling bad enough already. His silent treatment was deafening, and I felt like it was a double punishment.

By this stage of my life, I was not just acting out and getting into trouble for the sake of it. It was a cry for help. I was a teenager burning at both ends and I felt like he was giving up on me. He was present as a father, as he always had been, but he was choosing to be absent in important ways. I resented him for that. He spoke through my mother and so I did too. He kept his distance and I kept mine. Our relationship deteriorated and the driving lessons stopped. I would resume them a year later with my mother as my new instructor.

10

As fragile as an egg

AS FRAGILE AS AN EGG

There's a saying that goes, 'The first generation builds it, the second one makes it a success, and the third one loses it.' It's a Chinese proverb that is frequently bandied about in business circles and it speaks of how generational wealth is often lost in the hands of the succeeding generation because of a lack of trust and a lack of adequate training from the preceding generation. At the core of this adage lies a classic principle of management: what you don't manage you soon lose. It also speaks to every aspect of our lives. What you don't tend soon wilts right before your eyes.

But as painful as it may sound, some things do have to die for something new and better to be born. When something starts to eat into itself, when it turns gangrenous or cancerous, it is time for it to die. The first time I was confronted with this tough reality was when I was doing my second year of study at the Tshwane University of Technology. My mother called me one week out of the blue and asked me to come home for the weekend as she had something to discuss with me. My parents hardly ever called to check up on me during my varsity days. Normally I was the one who did the calling, mostly to ask for some more money around the middle of the month, so I knew that whatever she wanted to discuss with me had to be important.

I came home by train on a Friday afternoon. I was glad to be back. My baby brother Tumelo was not around. I figured that he was probably at my paternal grandmother's house or at my Aunty Dolly's place for a weekend visit. My mother told me to get some rest.

'We'll talk in the morning,' she said.

My father and I talked a little about my progress at varsity. Our relationship hadn't improved much since high school. Our engagements were mostly about surface stuff from his side with curt one-word responses from my side.

In the morning we all went about our business as usual,

running errands and doing chores. I then went to check up on some friends of mine.

In the afternoon my mother called me into her room. She asked me to close the door behind me. 'Come have a seat on the bed,' she said. She pulled out her phone and made me listen to a voice note message.

It was from some woman from Mabopane who claimed that my father was not taking care of a child that he had supposedly fathered with her.

'I have tried numerous times to get him to take responsibility for our little one with no success. That's why I have turned to you for help. I know that he is a married man, and he is happy with his family, but all I want is for him to help me with the baby,' she said.

I listened to the voice note about three times, trying to make sense of what I was hearing. She sounded genuine, like someone really pleading for help. It was not the voice of a young, naive girl. It was the voice of a mature woman in her mid thirties or early forties who, I presume, knew what she had been getting herself into in the first place.

Was she just trying to break up a happy home, I wondered, and where had she got my mother's number? What does she stand to gain from all of this? Did I really have a baby sister or brother somewhere in Mabopane? My father did like going to Mabopane over weekends to watch soccer games at the Odi Stadium, but were those soccer outings really an opportunity for him to engage in an extra-marital affair? Was it an old flame perhaps, from his time as a student there? I had so many questions swirling in my head.

My father had always preached the importance of taking responsibility for one's actions. Why would he make the mistake of impregnating someone outside of marriage? He was the one who always warned me to use a condom. And if he had in fact made this woman pregnant I just couldn't see him denying his own seed, his own flesh and blood, no matter how bad things got. I just could not see my father as that type of a person.

I was confused and hurt. My mother was defeated. She was at a point where she had seen it all and heard it all and now she was tired. Too tired to fight and scream. She had endured so much in her 25 years of marriage to my father that she no longer had any energy left in her. She did not even have the willpower to try to prove or to disprove the woman's claims.

She called my father into the room. She played the voice note again. My father just stood there, visibly upset. I do not know if it was because of what was being said on the voice note or because my mother had made me listen to it. But he was clearly upset. I suppose at being ambushed like that.

'Is it true?' I asked him.

He shook his head.

My eyes panned to our family portrait. It hung right above their bed.

'I don't know this woman. I have never heard of this woman and, no, I do not have an outside child somewhere. I think it's just people hellbent on hurting us as a family,' he said, pleadingly.

My mother walked out. My father fell silent. I just sat there on the bed. A few minutes later my mother walked in again.

'I've been through so much with this man. All the abuse, the cheating, the lack of respect, the silent treatments. Yes that's abuse too. That can destroy a person too,' she said. She told me he was even physically abusive to her, without going into detail.

My father shook his head, as if my mother was making all this up.

I knew that they had marriage problems like any other couple. I knew that in raising us some focus had to be shifted away from the marriage. I knew that a week wouldn't go by without the two of them arguing. They fought openly and sometimes they would take their arguments to the bedroom. I knew that their communication wasn't great. I knew that their marriage was far from perfect. But they made things work together. Making things work was their love language, I thought, and not this over-the-top soapie-inspired kind of love. So I always imagined that, as imperfect as they were, they would find a way to soldier on, just as they had picked up the pieces and moved on after losing Tshepo.

I wondered if me being away at varsity had anything to do with how things were unravelling. Had my time away from home amplified the cracks that had already formed in their marriage?

My mother composed herself and sat next to me.

'Marriage is like an egg, Tumiso,' she said to me, calmly and philosophically. 'If you keep hurting an egg, then soon enough it will crack. The cracks get bigger and bigger, until the egg breaks, and once an egg is broken then there's nothing anyone can do. You cannot undo the damage.'

'All these years I have been sacrificing for the family by staying in this marriage, but I cannot do this any longer,' she said.

My father just stood there quietly.

'So should I still stay in this marriage or leave? Tumelo is still a baby. He won't understand much of what is going on right now,' she asked.

The room fell quiet as I thought. I glanced at our family portrait again. It seemed unbelievable to me that their 25 years of marriage had now been reduced to me having to decide if they should carry on or not. I knew little about marriage but I knew how it feels to be a prisoner of memory and of sentiment. You are free but you are not really free. I also knew that marriage should not only be built on blood, sweat and tears but also on love, friendship, respect and trust. What I did not know then was that it can take years to build a house but just one careless, swinging move with a wrecking ball to bring it all down in an instant, and this is what was unfolding at that very moment. It was all coming down.

When I looked at my parents I saw two people who were trapped, two people who wanted to break free but who had no courage to do so, and that's when it hit me that this marriage had to die.

'So, should I stay in this marriage or should I leave?' my mother asked me again.

It was as if she had been coaching me for years for this moment. My mother and I had gone through so many stages in our relationship and we were now more like confidantes or comrades fighting side by side in battle. We could talk openly about anything. No son ever wants to see his mother hurting and no mother ever wants to see her son hurting, and at that point my mother was hurting. By asking me that question she was in effect placing a gun in my hand and all I had to do was pull the trigger. I was still angry and disappointed with my father. I blamed him for every bad thing that had ever happened to our family and I hated him even more now for putting himself first with what seemed to be his selfish actions. At that moment I felt nothing for him, absolutely nothing. I felt as if he was the common denominator in all of our problems as a family. So I pulled the trigger.

'Mama, you can leave this marriage. It's OK. You have my blessing,' I said point-blank.

When I gave my mother my blessing to leave the marriage I was not thinking about the devastating effects that a divorce can have on a family and I was thinking even less about what this might do to Tumelo, who was nine years old at the time. I was thinking about my anger and my hatred towards my father. I was also thinking about my mother's woes, all these years, stuck in a loveless, psychologically and, according to her, physically abusive marriage.

Not to discount the true experiences of women, particularly in South Africa, who suffer from gender-based violence every day, it's honestly not something that I had thought about deeply when it came to my parents' marriage. The revelation of physical abuse in the marriage came to me only on that day, when the divorce was being decided. I had never seen my father raise a hand to my mother, no matter how angry he got. My mother always came across as a strong woman who stood up for herself. But who is to say that women who seem outwardly strong cannot be victims of gender-based violence and cannot carry the trauma in silence?

The look on my father's face was one of sheer disappointment. He was absolutely shocked by what I had just said. It was as if I had just betrayed him. But I did not care. I had just chosen my mother over everything else, over the family and over him. I felt like I had finally gotten my revenge for the pain and suffering he had inflicted on me all these years. Blood was dripping from the dagger I had just plunged into his heart and I was relishing the moment.

My mother hugged me tightly and she told me that everything was going to be OK. I think her mind had already been made up. But she still needed me to be the one who pulled the trigger, she still needed my father to hear it come from my mouth, from his son.

I had come to a stable home on a Friday, but I left as a child from a broken home on the Sunday when I returned to varsity.

———

I went through the remainder of my second year at varsity with a sense of restlessness, a feeling of winding down. I was doing a four-year degree, two years full time and the other two part time, with a dissertation submission at the end. My two full-time years were coming to an end and I no longer felt like being at varsity or at res. By the end of the year I had no real home to go back to. My mother had moved out. It was just me, my father and my baby brother Tumelo. My mother would come by sometimes to check up on us. She was moving from place to place, trying to sort out her life. She kept some of her belongings, clothes and furniture, in the care of family and friends.

I spent the better part of those holidays out partying with friends and coming back home only to sleep at night. There was nothing that my father could say or do to me. He had forsaken his moral high ground by having an extra-marital affair. That December we all celebrated Christmas and New Year's Eve at different places and with different people. Broken up.

―――

Even though my father was bitter he was still hopeful that my mother would come back one day.

'Your mother is mad, that one. She needs to really stop this behaviour of hers,' he would tell me in passing. In his mind she was going through some silly mid-life crisis and she needed to snap out of it. It was only in May of the new year, when my mother bought herself a big, three-bedroomed, face-brick house in Etwatwa, Daveyton, that my father realised that she was never coming back.

I had never seen or heard my father cry, not even when Tshepo passed away. But one night after we had all gone to bed I heard him cry out, painfully and desperately, from his room. I could hear him try to suppress the cry but the emotion he was feeling must have been just too intense for him to stop. I think that night was his breaking point. It was very uncomfortable to hear such an outpouring of grief from my father. It showed me that he was human after. I felt sorry for him. I wished that I could reach out to him. But there was nothing I could do. I couldn't burst into his room and ask him if he was OK.

His moment of vulnerability felt important, as if he were coming to terms with all that he had kept shrouded up inside of him all these years. I could not take that away from him, as painful as it was to hear a grown man bawling.

A FATHER IS BORN

I also could not undo the past. I could not go back in time and tell my mother to give her marriage a second try. My blessing on her decision to leave the marriage and to forge a new life without my father could not be undone. In the morning we just went about our lives as usual.

At first my father tried to hold on to the house, but he was struggling to keep up with the repayments on his own. So he and my mother, who were married in community of property, agreed to sell the house and to split the proceeds equally while their divorce was being finalised. The two had resolved to be amicable with each other for the sake of me and Tumelo.

But the one thing that my father was not prepared to compromise on was Tumelo. He told my mother that there was no way she was going to get full custody of him. He told her that her life was unstable and she was not going to unsettle Tumelo's life as well. I had now moved out of home and was trying to make it in the media industry as a working young man in the busy streets of Johannesburg. So I was the least of my father's concerns. Tumelo was the only person he had left, and he was determined to hold on to him no matter what. He was also determined to give him a stable home and to ensure that his schooling was not interrupted.

My mother did try to get full custody, but my father was adamant that it was not going to happen. He was actually quite threatening. He did not say in so many words what he might do if my mother continued to try to gain full custody. But one could deduce from his language and tone that he meant business, and that he was prepared to do anything to stop Tumelo being taken away from him.

My father's attitude towards my mother had now evolved into sheer hatred. He stopped referring to her as 'your mother' and started calling her 'that one'. At the time my father had a 9 mm calibre firearm and my mother feared that if he were to be pushed to the limits he might be tempted to use it, and so she relented and agreed to see Tumelo only on weekends.

But bitter and angry as he was, my father used this period to get right as a parent with my little brother Tumelo what he got wrong with me and Tshepo. At first, after the old house was sold, he moved to a flat with Tumelo. A few months later he bought a big stand-alone house, which would become Tumelo's new and permanent home. My father's life now revolved only around his work as the principal of Sechaba Primary School and around Tumelo's needs and well-being. In a sense he was actually now the sole parent because my mother was still figuring out her new life.

My father attended all the parent-teacher meetings at Tumelo's school. My mother would be present only sometimes. He supported Tumelo's extra-curricular activities too. They went on holidays together to places like Durban and Cape Town. When Sechaba had outings, he would take Tumelo along with him.

And he never raised a hand against him. Not even once. He nurtured him with nothing but positivity. He cooked for him every day. He helped him with his schoolwork. He framed all his merit and achievement certificates and he proudly hung them up on the walls around the new house. I started warming to him. He was no longer the same father that had raised me and Tshepo. He was maturing into a better father. Everyone deserves a second chance, I thought.

―――

While my mother's divorce from my father was still being finalised, she began seeing this dark-skinned fellow named Liwa who worked at the Carnival City Casino in Boksburg. My mother's sister Aunty Dolly never hid from my mother how much she disliked the new man in her life.

'He's so ugly,' she would quip whenever she had the chance.

But my mother didn't care. She was determined to show everybody that she could move on without my father.

It was strange for me at first seeing her with a man other than my father, and he was slightly younger too. So I wondered if she was going through a mid-life crisis. But I figured that maybe it was her way of trying to get over my father quickly after years and years of marriage. He was just a temporary fix, a distraction in that season of her life, so I thought it best to let her be. I never liked the guy much though. I saw him as *Rra Baiki*, a man who comes into a new relationship with only his jacket and leaves with the same jacket once the relationship ends. Thankfully the relationship didn't last very long. One night, in a drunken state, the man rolled my mother's bakkie and he didn't have the money to fix it. Their relationship ended shortly thereafter.

But in no time at all she began seeing Nic, a former policeman, I presume, and a true gentleman at heart. I presume that he was a former policeman because one day he suggested that the car I was driving at the time, a grey hatchback Opel Kadett of the kind popularly known as a 'Bon Jovi' in the townships, could've been previously owned by a policeman because of how the one side of the driver's seat had been worn out. He said that type of wear and tear was usually due to the butt of the gun in the holster constantly rubbing up against the seat.

Nic was pretty handy. He helped my mother around the house with whatever needed to be fixed and with her businesses also. I was suspicious of him at first because of how perfect he was. I thought that maybe he was there just to take my mother for a ride. I was also concerned that my mother was moving too fast from one relationship to the next. Was she trying to make up for lost time, I wondered. Did she feel that her youth had been taken away somehow by my father, leaving her with the need to cover as much lost ground as possible? But I was also becoming less judgemental and less idealistic generally. So again, I let her be.

Fortunately, Nic turned out to be a genuine guy who was indeed looking for companionship. The two of them would date for a long while and my mother would later help him establish his own funeral parlour business. I could see that she was happy and so I was happy for her.

My parents' divorce was finalised on 18 September 2003, bringing to an end a love affair that had begun 30 years before when my father, still a hopeful young man, first whistled for my mother, still a naive schoolgirl, to stop for some small talk. For a long time I wondered if I had played a hand in ending my parents' marriage based solely on my own anger. What if my father was telling the truth that day he was confronted with the voice note? What if he ended up paying for a misdeed that he never committed? What if that voice note was indeed bogus as he had claimed?

We had not actively sought out the truth of that voice note, after all. Yet we acted. My mother and me. We acted on an untested voice note that had a five-day lifespan on her Nokia 3210 before it was automatically deleted from the phone's storage. There were no letters, bank statements or phone records to suggest that my father may have been secretly supporting an illegitimate child somewhere, and no half-brother or half-sister came knocking at the door on the day of his funeral to claim his or her rightful place in the family.

Of course I wondered if I had perhaps robbed my brother Tumelo of a full family life. What if I was wrong all along and what if my father suffered for nothing, for something that was baseless? What if I had played a hand in destroying our family only because of the hatred and anger that I felt for him at the time? How could I ever look Tumelo in the eye and claim to have his best interests at heart as a big brother if I was party to such a misdeed in his life? My mother's mind had indeed been made up about leaving my father. But she still needed me to be the one who rubber-stamped it. I could not undo my part in all of this, but I wondered for a long while how things would've turned out if we had just paused for a second or two that Saturday afternoon instead of acting out on emotion.

Some years after my father passed on, my mother would tell me that she actually regretted going ahead with the divorce. Maybe she was feeling sentimental, maybe she was missing her first love and the father of her children and maybe life as a divorcee was much harder than she had anticipated. But she was genuinely remorseful at the decision she had taken. If given another chance she would have definitely tried to make her marriage work again, she told me.

There's a saying in Setswana which goes, '*Molato hao bole.*' It means, 'One's misdeeds, if left unanswered or unaccounted for, will always catch up with one.' Loosely, one's misdeeds never rot; the flesh of the dead may rot, but never their misdeeds, even in the grave.

Some years later, while I was sifting through old family photos, I found a letter addressed to my father from a certain Maggie in Vereeniging. The letter, which had been sent to his work address, was framed with little hearts, and there was a picture enclosed of the slender-framed and bespectacled Maggie, who was probably in her mid forties.

The letter read:

Hello Neo. Thank you very much for your letter. I received it on Tuesday. So, you have not told me about yourself. Please will you tell me, because I don't want to take chances. Neo, if you are serious then you will respond immediately. I am serious. How many kids do you have? I enclosed my photo and I'm looking forward to [having] yours too. Honey, I really mean it. You won't be disappointed.

Yours sincerely
Maggie

At first I didn't make much of the letter. I figured that it was his way of trying to get back into the dating game after he and my mother had separated. I also thought that it was cute of him to go the old-school 'pen-pal' route. This was way before online dating sites were popular.

But on closer inspection, I saw that the letter was dated 27 July 1999. I was still in high school then and the accusation that he had fathered a child outside of marriage hadn't been made yet.

He never did make the mistake of bringing this letter back home with him. He wouldn't dare be so reckless, I imagined. Instead, the letter was sent to us, along with all his other personal belongings, by his work colleagues who cleared his office after he had passed. The truth or fragments of the truth always have a way of coming out, it seems.

II

A family gathering

A FAMILY GATHERING

In my family we gather mostly when there is a death in the family, a cleansing ceremony following a death in the family or a tombstone of a family member that has to be unveiled. So death more than life is what brings us together. But when we do converge now, it's hardly ever sombre. It's usually warm and merry and sometimes even comical.

In April of 2005 I received a phone call from my baby cousin Tshidi. 'Koko is not well,' she told me. From her tone I could tell that my paternal grandmother's condition was grave. She had been in and out of hospital for the last couple of months and she had been taking medication upon medication, but she still wasn't getting any better. At 76 years old, she was at a stage in her life where one ailment automatically led to another, so I could sense that this might be the only opportunity that I had left to see her while she was still alive.

'OK, I will see you tomorrow after work,' I said.

The following day I picked up my brother Tumelo in the afternoon, and then we headed to my grandmother's place.

By the time we arrived a big part of me had accepted that if she were to go then I would be fine with it. So I was jovial when Tumelo and I walked in. Looking after my grandmother was Tshidi, my other cousin Mmapule and my aunt M'shala. Tshidi's younger sister Happy was not around. She was probably around and about in the streets. Tshidi, Mmapule and M'shala all looked fatigued and out of hope. They were now just waiting. Waiting for the inevitable. I probably commented on how Tshidi was looking more and more like her beautiful late mother Maniki, especially with her big eyes, and I probably made gentle fun of Mmapule's big cheeks and her humanly impossible knock-knees that were forever caught up in a steamy embrace. And she probably hit back with how fat I was getting or how short I still was in comparison to all the tall men in the family, and she also probably delighted in how well-mannered Tumelo was and how big he was growing. M'shala, who was always in an offish mood, even when an occasion demanded otherwise, probably asked me about my mother and how she was doing. At the time she actually held ill-feelings towards my mother for divorcing my father, so I probably responded with a glowing account.

When I walked into my grandmother's room she was sleeping on her bed. But it was more like she was in a daze, like one who was there but not really there. She was somewhere between the land of the living and of those who had passed on. Mmapule brought out some chairs for us to sit on. M'shala busied herself with something. I don't know what exactly. Tshidi brought us some water to drink and then she made herself comfortable on the edge of my grandmother's bed. We spoke for about 30 minutes before Tshidi remarked with a mischievous smile on how shy and quiet Tumelo was.

'He's just like that,' I said.

Tumelo, the most awkward introvert I know, especially when he is around people, avoided eye contact and instead looked towards the bare, cream-white walls of my grandmother's room for some cover, any kind of cover, but none was forthcoming. The spotlight had turned on him and he could feel our eyes.

'Can he speak Sotho or does he only speak English?' asked Tshidi, again with a mischievous smile

'Ask him,' I said, as a way of trying to include my brother in the conversation.

But Tumelo just smiled and nodded shyly as he usually does.

My grandmother awoke from her daze. She sat up on her bed. The room fell quiet. I wondered if maybe we were too loud for her. We greeted her but she couldn't make us out. She was in a state of delirium and experiencing serious pain. Her face was gaunt. Her skin had lost so much of its elasticity. It was sagging and her complexion was lifeless and grey. Her hands were swollen. 'It's from all the years she was working with water as a

A FAMILY GATHERING

domestic worker,' I remembered M'shala once telling me.

My grandmother muttered something that only Tshidi could make out. From where I was sitting it looked like speaking took too much of her energy. So I did not engage her at all. Tshidi grabbed an ointment tube from the bedside table and cosied up next to Koko. She lifted the back of her pyjama top, applied the ointment to her back and rubbed it in thoroughly. I could see some relief come over my grandmother's face.

I glanced at Tumelo. He was absolutely horrified by how my grandmother was looking and I could see that he wanted to cry. During my parents' separation process my father used to drop Tumelo off with my grandmother whenever he had an urgent engagement. So the two of them had grown very close. I could understand why he was so emotional. As I sat there quietly, I reflected on my own past times with my grandmother. I remembered how loving and caring she was. She was always so protective over me. She always kept me close to her and she didn't want me to wander about on my own whenever I came over for a visit. She loved to have me on her lap in the kitchen next to the Welcome Dover coal stove and to feed me with fruit and sweets while she conversed with visiting family and friends or with M'shala's beer customers. I don't remember ever being scolded by her. She was always so happy to see me and she would always give me whatever little money she had in her purse.

She fell asleep again. Tshidi turned to us with a sigh and with a look of deep worry in her eyes. She had lost her mother, Maniki, some years ago and now it seemed she was about to lose Koko as well. Tumelo and I left soon after that.

―――

The following week I received another phone call from Tshidi. This time around it was to inform me that Koko had passed on. I did not cry, nor was I sad. I was actually happy that her pain was

A FATHER IS BORN

now over. It would have been way too soon to bury her the next weekend, and quite a number of people were expected to attend her funeral, so we also couldn't have it on a weekday. I have family who live in far-flung places like Middelburg, Tafelkop and Burgersfort, so it only made sense that we delay her burial until the following weekend.

My grandmother's last-born child Thabo, a handsome and a tall man with a commanding baritone voice, brought along his two children Refilwe and Mmatsatsi to help out in the house ahead of the funeral. I'm told that he then convened an impromptu meeting in the kitchen where he told everyone present that he was going to take care of the groceries and the meat and that he was also going to organise a high-flying metro police convoy to ensure that Koko's send-off went without a hitch. He assured them that the convoy would be green-lighted with no problem at all because he was very active in the ANC structures of his community. I'm also told that this was the last they saw or heard from him until the day before the funeral, when he as the last-born in the family had to lie next to my grandmother in her coffin for a few seconds as tradition and culture dictated.

My grandmother's third-born son, Mbuti, a bony and a lanky man whose facial features had taken a knock over the years as a result of his excessive drinking of alcohol, arrived from Burgersfort in Limpopo a few days later, after my grandmother had passed. Mbuti worked as a drill operator in one of the platinum mines in that part of the world. He said he would've come sooner but his managers at work were giving him a hard time with approving his compassionate leave. He said they only approved it late, after he promised them that he would bring back a copy of the death certificate. But I suspect that he honestly didn't have any money to come to Springs and had to borrow some just to make the trip. I suspect that he also didn't have any money to make the trip back after the funeral.

I'm told that when he arrived at my grandmother's house he kept following his baby sister M'shala around and asking her, 'So what's happening? What's the plan?' with a sense of urgency in his voice. But M'shala, my grandmother's youngest daughter and the last surviving girl child, was just dismissive of him. She felt that instead of him asking, 'So what's happening? What's the plan?' all the time he should've looked around to see what was missing and then taken the initiative to sort it out. She viewed Mbuti as a good-for-nothing big brother who prioritised the bottle over everything else. The irony, though, is that every time Mbuti is in town he always makes sure that he buys his beers from M'shala and that his drinking buddies do the same. In the end Mbuti offered to take care of the buses that were to ferry people from the house to the church, then to the graveyard and then back again. Not much hope was placed in that offer, nor was it ever fulfilled. He also made a promise to M'shala that he would refrain from drinking alcohol until after the funeral as a sign of respect for their mother. He didn't keep that promise either.

But Mbuti wasn't always like this. In his heyday he was a dashing and a well-dressed man. He was part of the 1980s township sub-culture called the 'Ivy'. The Ivies were swanky and suave. They wore the latest fashion of the day, like two-tone Florsheim shoes and fedora hats, and they did not have any problem at all with the opposite sex, unlike their fiercest rivals, the Pantsulas.

My grandmother's third-born child, my father, who was the de facto big brother in the family and the only one with a car, did most of the running around when it came to the funeral arrangements. From our telephone conversations that week I could tell that he was highly stressed. Fortunately my grandmother had a funeral policy and her church card was up to date. A church card is paid monthly by the congregants so as to ensure that in the event of their passing the church will bury them. But if you skip a month or two then the church might or might not bury you. So the big things like the casket, the tent, the funeral cortege, the plot where she was going to be buried and the catering were already taken care of. It was the little things like the day-to-day groceries, the petrol for his up and down trips, the flowers and the printing of the funeral programmes, for example, that had him all stressed out, little things that added up in the end. I could not get off work because a grandmother, strangely enough, was not considered part of one's immediate family as per company policy. So I sent my father R2000 instead, as my way of chipping in towards the funeral.

The three brothers Thabo, Mbuti and my father were all divorcees at the time of my grandmother's passing. But their ex-wives – Ouma, Grace and my mother respectively – showed up at the house, head-wrapped and with their shoulders well covered, to help out in whatever way they could, for in their eyes *Ousie* Pina was still their mother. They took turns to sit on the mattress with my grandmother's sisters to help them mourn and to receive messages of condolence from the people who kept trickling in every day. They also all helped out around the house with the endless cooking and cleaning. In the eyes of the family they were still regarded as *dingwetsi tsa ga* Mashaba – the women of Mashaba – and they were all embraced as such. My mother even helped my father with some money towards the funeral.

Theirs had been a union that my grandmother had always believed in, especially after Tshepo's passing. She held their marriage in high regard, and she was completely against the idea of a divorce. She had urged my mother several times not to go ahead with it. But in the end there was nothing she could do but accept my mother's decision. As final as death is, it is also revealing. My grandmother's death revealed to me that family will always be family, no matter what a divorce paper decrees.

A FAMILY GATHERING

The day of Koko's funeral was bright and shiny. Her open casket was placed in the living room. We all had a turn to see her for the last time. Her face looked pale, stiffened and sorrowful and unlike the grandmother I had known. Tshidi cried bitterly when she saw her.

Mbuti asked me, as the eldest male grandchild, to be one of the pallbearers who would carry my grandmother's coffin from the house to the hearse outside.

'No problem,' I told him. I felt good about being given such a task.

When we left the house for the Evangelical Lutheran Church, where my grandmother's funeral service was to be held, there was no metro police convoy in sight, but there was, to my surprise, a full marching band in front of the departing funeral cortege. They played gloriously. Tshidi was part of the band, and her boyfriend at the time and now-husband Bheki was the band's leader. She had asked him if he could organise a little something for her grandmother's send-off. The marching band helped to change the complexion of the funeral from sad and heavy to celebratory.

The Evangelical Lutheran Church, in my opinion, is a church that is still very conservative in its ways. It is completely unlike the modern-day oval-shaped, double-storey auditorium churches that have theatre seats and cinema-size monitors in the front, where congregants are free to praise and worship in whatever way the spirit leads them, and where the pastors don't look a day over 40. It's an orthodox church. Its design is Georgian-inspired. It has a high-pitched roof, a big church bell hoisted up above the entrance and stained glass windows. The hymns are sung in a monotonous tone following a dull melody, and the preaching style, in my opinion, is just as off-colour as the praising and worshipping. But oddly the appeal of the church has not wavered over the years, especially for the younger generation, who cannot wait their turn to wear the church's black and white uniform.

I don't remember much of my grandmother's funeral service except for the part towards the end when the women of the church, dressed in the uniform, got up from their seats and sang, '*Tumelo ke Thebe* – My belief is my shield'. It was the most rousing and spirit-lifting rendition of the hymn I have ever heard. At one point the women vacated their seats and formed a human train that went all around the church, and just when you thought they had surely reached the end of the hymn the lead would belt out, '*Ke tsamaya le Jeso* – I will forever walk with Jesus,' once more, and the singing would continue. It was a fitting tribute to my grandmother, and for a second or two I reconsidered my position on the church. It was in this very church that she had witnessed the funeral services of her husband Tshungwane, her grandchild Tshepo and her daughter Maniki, and now it was her turn.

Koko was laid to rest in the same plot at the old Kwa-Thema cemetery as my grandfather, who had passed on 19 years before. Initially I thought that we were going to take a long time with the closing up of her grave, or their grave I should say, but all the young men from my grandmother's street and from her church worked the shovels with great determination and it went very quickly. I got in one turn with the shovel if I'm not mistaken.

My father then gave the vote of thanks. In my family, this assignment is usually delegated to my father's cousin-brother Uncle Ronnie. But I suppose that my father wanted to be the one who got to have the final say on this occasion. I think that my grandmother was the only person who really understood him, at least from his point of view. The two of them were very close. My grandfather passed away in 1986 from a respiratory disease. So, over the years my father was the one who always made sure that my grandmother was well looked after.

He tended to all of her needs, taking her to the hospital, looking after her phone bill, making sure that she always had food to eat and generally seeing to it that she never lacked for anything. I don't recall what he said exactly but I do recall how passionate and how proud he was of the race my grandmother had run while she was still alive, speaking all the while in his pitch-perfect Setswana. 'A ene pula – Let it rain,' he called out in closing. As we left the graveyard the heavens opened in reply.

Traditionally speaking, funeral-goers are only supposed to be fed with a basic plate of food such as samp and meat, and the food is not supposed to be cooked with salt, to symbolise the sad nature of the occasion. But those beliefs are hardly ever practised, especially in the townships. Mourners at my grandmother's funeral were fed with the typical seven or several colours Sunday meal. The starch options were samp, rice, pap or *ting* (mabele porridge). The options of *sishebo*, or sauces and mains, were creamed spinach, tomato gravy, onion soup, beef curry and fried chicken. The choice of vegetables included steamed carrots, pumpkin and beetroot, and there was a variety of salads as well. The food was delicious, just like the food they normally serve at weddings.

Rrangwane Mbuti walked up to me after I had eaten, and he sparked up a light conversation about what still needed to be sorted out around the house. Then he grabbed my arm and asked for some beer money.

'You are working now, and I've never seen a cent from you. So please make a plan. You can see that I'm struggling,' he said.

Mbuti was the kind of uncle that was always going on at me, whether it be about me forgetting to call him *Rrangwane* or me not being able to speak Sepedi. He always gave me a hard time, but playfully so. I could tell that there was no way he was going to let go of my arm until I gave him something. I could also tell that he had already had his own after tears before the actual after tears. 'Let me see what I can do,' I said, and he loosened his grip. It was a classic shake-down, involving application of firm physical contact and clever use of emotive language. I withdrew a R20 note from my wallet and gave it to him. He didn't look too pleased, but he took the money, nonetheless.

My father, who was nowhere to seen, called me on my phone and asked me if we could please meet up on Kgaswane Road, the main road not so far from my grandmother's house. When I got there, I parked my car and walked across to his bottle green Toyota Camry. I climbed in the passenger side.

'Thank you for coming,' he said. He explained the clandestine meeting. 'I called you here because there are some people at the house that I'm trying to avoid. People that I really don't want to talk to.'

'That reminds me ... some people at the house are asking for copies of the death certificate. I told them that I would talk to you about it,' I said.

'What people?' he asked, displeased.

'Just family,' I said.

He chuckled.

'Never give copies of a death certificate to just anyone,' he said.

'But why?' I asked him, curious.

'Because some people use death certificates for fraud,' he said.

'But why would someone like Mbuti want to do fraud?'

'Don't worry, I will sort Mbuti out with a copy. But always be mindful of who comes to you and asks for such things. Some people open policies without you knowing anything about it. Maybe they opened policies under Koko's name, and we knew nothing about it, and now they want to cash in,' he said.

I just nodded, still a little confused.

'I wanted to thank you for the R2000. It went a long way. Thank you so much,' he said, with pride in his eyes.

'Sure. No problem,' I said. It wasn't a big deal for me. I was working and I felt that I was being responsible with my money by helping out family in a time of need.

'You have no idea how much that money came in handy. None of your uncles contributed anything towards the funeral. It was all me. They did absolutely nothing. So honestly, thank you very much for your contribution,' he said.

'Nothing?' I asked.

'When I say nothing I mean nothing,' he said with a serious face.

I felt good about myself. I felt as if I had finally done something to earn his approval. I could not help but feel important for that R2000 I had contributed. But giving money and actually 'being there' are two different things and all I did really was to give money towards my grandmother's funeral. That's all. Still, I felt glad that my father had taken the time to call me aside and thank me personally for having stepped up as a young working man. I was happy that we could finally talk so openly, man to man, about sensitive things like money that break families apart.

Later I realised that the way he went about the preparations for his mother's funeral was all about reasserting his importance in the family. As much as he was the big brother and the one who had to ensure that everything was taken care of, his siblings genuinely did not have any money. It was not that they felt less for their mother than he did. They just did not have anything to give, and this was a message that was impossible to get through to my father. My grandmother passed away in the middle of the month, when no one had money. But my father was a self-righteous man and I suspect that his siblings felt that they could not reach out to him and possibly find a better working relationship that did not necessarily need money.

I don't think he gave any of them a chance. He was stubborn in his ways and thinking, and that's why the siblings could never all be under one roof together to discuss together how they were going to bury their mother. As much they could not stand each other generally, they could not stand my father more. My father, who didn't touch alcohol, also felt that they prioritised the bottle over everything else.

He was a man who carried his self-importance proudly, and I think he could not let such a big occasion slip past without asserting himself. People tend to hold back when they are confronted with a strong, vain personality, and I think this is exactly what happened. My father's siblings held back, and they let him run the show. Blinded by his inflated sense of self and the idea that no one could possibly love his mother more than him, he basked in his own glory.

PART 4

12

The possibility of just being …

A FATHER IS BORN

I long for the possibility of romance that lingers on long after the physical attraction has gone, a possibility of mutual respect with that special someone that's beyond class, race or 'age', a possibility of that baby boy or girl to add smiles and cheers and to make life worthwhile, a possibility of that farm I want and that house at Hartbeespoort Dam, a possibility of holidaying without a care in the world, a possibility of just being ...

Apparently, this poem, sent via SMS on New Year's Day in 2007 to Elrees, who was just a work colleague of mine at the time, is what sealed the deal for me. I had been pursuing her for some months.

She was someone I used to bump into in the corridors of the SABC where I was working as a news producer. She was a beautiful lady with striking Cape Malayan features, who hailed from Ennerdale, south of Johannesburg. She had a lemon-tinged complexion, high cheekbones, a straight-edged nose, a welcoming gap-toothed smile and thick, flowing, curly black hair. She always used to greet me with a lovely, bright smile. Later I would learn that she used to work at SABC Tours, where she was responsible for taking school kids on field trips around the building, so greeting people in general with a lovely, bright smile was just part of her job. I was not special at all. I had no clue then how deeply intertwined our destinies would be in the future.

My chance to get closer to her came when I was appointed as a current affairs producer at SAfm. At the time SAfm, the SABC's main English-language station, and Radio Sonder Grense (Radio Without Borders, the Afrikaans-language service) were sharing an open-plan office, and Elrees was working as a producer for the latter radio station. Her workstation was right next to the table where SAfm held its daily diary meetings. I was finding it difficult to get into the groove of things because in my previous job at Channel Africa, the SABC's international radio service, my focus had been mainly on African issues. The pace of delivery had also

THE POSSIBILITY OF JUST BEING ...

been much slower because the shows I had produced only went on air once a week. At SAfm, however, the focus was on South African socio-political issues, and the shows had to go on air every day of the week.

My engagements in these diary meetings were limited. I knew that Elrees was often listening, and because I liked her I kept my contributions to a minimum, lest she think that I was just some clueless guy who had got into SAfm via the back door. But I couldn't keep that up if I wanted to stay employed. So I brushed up on my local news sense and general knowledge, and I started participating more and more in these diary meetings. But I was still a long way from home.

One day I took a chance, and sent her an email asking her how long she had been in radio. I couldn't just walk up to her desk and start chatting her up. That was way too risky. What if she shut me down and the whole office saw? I couldn't take that chance. So, emails were a safer bet.

'Just a little under 19 months. Why?' she responded about ten minutes later.

'It just seems like you take your work in your stride, like most people in this office. It's like second nature to you. Meanwhile every day is a learning curve for me,' I replied.

'Don't worry, you'll get into the hang of things sooner than you think. I've been there. I know the feeling. Shout if I can do something to help,' she responded towards close of business.

From then on I could just walk up to her and talk to her without worrying about prying eyes around the office. But I still needed an 'in'.

Soon she found out that I had access to the SABC's recorded music library, and she asked if I could draw some CDs for her. She was looking for Judith Sephuma's *A Cry, A Smile, A Dance* album, amongst others. That was my 'in', I thought. I wasted no time in drawing the CDs for her from the library. She was so thankful when I handed her the batch. But nothing came of that 'kind' act.

Some weeks later, the music library sent me an overdue notice for the CDs. I told Elrees about this and she told me that she was still using them. I said OK. A week later I received yet another overdue notice. She told me that she would bring the CDs to work the following day. The following day became the day after and the day after became the following week, and so it went. It got to a point where she was ducking and diving whenever she saw me. Watching her squirm and stumble over her words trying to explain the whereabouts of those CDs was priceless to me. I no longer needed an 'in'. I now had a 'hold'.

After some time, she brought back the CDs, but one was missing. It was the Judith Sephuma CD. Someone had nicked it from her car. She said she was going to try to get a replacement by month-end. Fortunately, she did. I wrote her an email thanking her for the CDs, and in it I told her about how much I enjoyed having this hold over her. I complimented her on the white blouse that she had on that day. I also told her that I thought she was cool and that she mustn't take that the wrong way.

'I obviously think you're cool too. Take that any way you like. I don't mind.' she responded.

I read that part over and over again, with a smile on my face and with a warm, fuzzy feeling in my heart.

We got to know each other a bit better around the office. I learnt that she once worked at a bank, she had hustled her way through varsity to get her degree and she had a car and her own place. She was the total package in my eyes. But apparently she liked me for her younger sister Sherelle, and she wanted to hook us up. I politely declined and I asked her out for coffee instead.

'I will do coffee with you. You must just let me know where and when,' she told me.

But we never got to it. Our times were always clashing.

On 23 October 2006, my former manager, Manzolwandle

Hadebe, came around to our office looking for Elrees, but she was not there. He asked me to please tell her to call him. When I told Elrees that Manzolwandle was looking for her she told me that it was because she was moving to Channel Africa as a bulletin compiler and presenter. I was a little sad that she was moving on just as we were getting to know each other. Even though she would still be in the same building, we would not be sharing office space.

On 20 November she asked me about that coffee we'd been meaning to have. She was leaving in a couple of days. We made plans to meet up in Melville but she had some brake issues with her car and we had to postpone.

On 26 November I emailed her about coffee and I told her that I had a going-away present for her. It was two tickets to see Joyous Celebration perform live. She loved the gesture.

'So, are we going?' she asked me.

I said no, she could take her sister instead. She liked the thought.

I was getting closer and closer. I just had to press on with my pursuit. But for the next three weeks I did nothing. No phone calls. No SMSs. No emails. Nothing. She was probably wondering why I had suddenly gone quiet on her. But I was being careful. She had just started a new job, so I was giving her some time to settle in. After a while though, I thought that this playing it cool thing was not working for me.

So on 28 December I sent her an email telling her about how much I was thinking about her and how much I was missing her.

'Stop being so sweet will you? Because I may start developing a crush for real,' she responded. She told me to ease up because she was turning 30 soon and it was not right that she was falling for a 25-year-old. But the age gap was immaterial to me. I had dated an older woman before. When I looked at her I saw more than just her age, I saw forever. I had known for a while that this was the woman that I wanted to be with for the rest of my life, and now that she was warming up to me I couldn't let the opportunity slip away.

The following day I asked her if we could meet up at the canteen downstairs. We were both awkward and shy. I don't remember much of what we said. But what I do remember is me saying that I wanted to take care of her. We hugged. It was a long hug.

'Only time will tell,' she said.

From that day on, we started chatting more and more on the phone.

In the New Year, on 5 January 2007, after I had sent her a poem about what type of future I envisioned for the two of us, we met up at a restaurant in Melville to officially have that coffee we'd been meaning to have. She wore her hair loose and curly that day. She had a fancy blouse on and a long Mexican-style skirt, and she looked just like Salma Hayek in my eyes. We had our coffee and we spoke about our wishes and dreams for the relationship. As we parted, outside the restaurant, we kissed for the first time.

'I don't know if I told you before, but I care for you. I go all mushy and sentimental when I think about you. When did this happen?' she wrote to me by email as soon as she got to the office.

They say when a man knows, he knows, and with Elrees, I knew. We both threw our weight behind the relationship. Instinctively we wanted to share each other's lives.

For her 30th birthday I took her to Sun City for a weekend getaway. It was just two months after we had started dating. Nothing breaks or makes a relationship more than a weekend getaway, especially when it's still early days in a relationship. It was a gamble. But I was in love and I was willing to take that risk. *Fortune favours the brave*, I thought. I booked us in at the President Paul Kruger Guest Lodge, which was not too far from Sun City. We left Joburg late in the afternoon on a Friday and arrived at the guest house that night. We had a cosy night's rest. In the morning we made our way to Sun City.

But just as we were about to pay the entrance fee my mother called me. She was in a state.

'Where are you?' she asked.

'I'm away. In the North West,' I told her.

'I'm at your place now and someone has broken in,' she said. 'You need to come back. Leaving the house like this will only invite more break-ins. I keep telling you to get burglar bars for your door, but you don't listen. You need to get here urgently.'

I hung up and explained what was going on to Elrees.

'We can always do Sun City. For now, you need to sort out your place,' she said.

We were right there and I wanted us to carry on. But she insisted that we drive back. She told me that I wasn't going to enjoy Sun City in any case, because my mind would be back at my place. We made a U-turn and headed back to Joburg.

I wanted to drop her off first, but she wanted to go with me for support. When we arrived at my house the wooden door was wide open. A window was broken too. The burglar had taken the DVD player, my desktop computer, my sneakers and some sheets, duvets and blankets. The TV was just too big to carry, I thought. I was demoralised. But I was glad Elrees was by my side.

The following morning my father came to check up on me. He walked in and found Elrees lazing on the couch, wearing her cheeky shorts and watching cricket. I was still busy with something in the bedroom. Elrees immediately got up from the couch, and she greeted my father as 'Mr Mashaba'.

'Where do you know me from?' my father asked with a surprised chuckle.

'From the pictures,' Elrees said.

She offered him a seat and asked if she could get him something to drink.

A FATHER IS BORN

'Water please,' he said.

I walked into the lounge and started chatting with my father. When Elrees came back from the kitchen I introduced her to my father. I had never introduced any of my girlfriends to my father, nor had I been planning to introduce Elrees. The situation had caught me by surprise. I wasn't expecting him at all. Normally he would come during the week to drop off my mail. Elrees and my father then got into a hearty conversation about cricket. I was surprised that he followed cricket and that he knew all the players. For a while I was invisible. Elrees would later tell me how uncomfortable she was because of the cheeky shorts she was wearing. She'd intended them for Sun City. But those were all the clothes she had with her, so there was nothing she could do about it.

When my father had finished his water, he got up and said his thanks and goodbyes and I walked him to the car. He was curious about the racial and cultural dynamics of our relationship and how we were planning on doing things. I told him that we were just dating for now. Nothing too serious. But he could tell that something serious could potentially develop and so he took it upon himself to give me his Four Pillars or Principles of Marriage. He was now a divorced man, and yet there he was giving marriage advice to someone who was not even thinking about marriage.

I indulged him all the same.

He broke it down: 'First it's communication. Communication can make or break a marriage. Then comes money. If one partner is not honest about money, for example, then that can really hurt your marriage. Thirdly it's the in-laws. No matter what you do, try not to involve the in-laws. That's the worst mistake that people make. Issues should always be resolved between the two of you.'

My father and I had never had the sex talk. Ever. Telling someone to always use a condom lest they make somebody pregnant is not a sex talk. It's a warning. So what came next was a little jarring.

'Finally it's sex. Sex is very important in a marriage. One cannot have good sex if the other three areas in a marriage are not in alignment,' he stressed.

I thanked him for his pearls of wisdom and bade him farewell, then went inside and told Elrees all about it. We had a good laugh.

13

A long way from home

From as far back as I can remember I always struggled with love relationships. Every time I got too close to somebody, I would find a way of sabotaging the relationship, doing things like cheating, disengaging or being plain old accusatory.

There was always something wrong. She was too skinny. She was not much of a talker. She was too much of a talker. She was secretive. She thought that she was God's gift to men. She had no sense of humour. She was too emotional. She was clingy. The list was endless.

But in truth I was the type of person who did not know how to open up, or how to love or let someone else love me, for that matter. How could I? I was struggling with loving and accepting myself to begin with, so how could I possibly love and accept someone else? I was always guarded with my emotions. I hardly ever spoke about myself – who I was, where I was from. My life story basically. I hated my life story. In relationships I was always the one listening, hardly ever talking about myself. I would ghost whoever it was, sooner or later, anyway. I would reject them before they could reject me.

My search was always outward when it should've been inward. Whatever flaw I was seeking to correct was usually not the other person's, but mine.

I think that my parents' marriage and their endless fights had a lot to do with it. When I was growing up, for example, I hardly ever saw my parents being affectionate and loving to one another. I don't recall ever seeing them holding hands. I don't remember any playful and loving conversations between them. The only time I ever saw them kissing was in their wedding day pictures.

Maybe my mother had been fine with how she and my father had chosen to express their love, quietly and behind closed doors, and maybe she had also been fine without showy, European-inspired overtures of love from my father, as long as he was present and taking care of his responsibilities. Maybe that, to her, was love. But I think that it would have been helpful if I had seen them being affectionate while I was growing up. I think maybe it would have positively shaped how I view love and how I love. To this day I still find it difficult to hold hands in public.

Even though I was trying to give my all in this new relationship with Elrees, at the core of my being was still a fractured and detached being. One who really did not know how to be in a relationship for longer than a year, who did not know how to forgive and who did not know how to compromise. I think I had always subconsciously prophesied that I was not going to be good in relationships, and my actions were invariably self-fulfilling.

In the days leading up to Elrees' 31st birthday I decided to break up with her.

'I want out,' I told her.

'What do you mean you want out?' she asked.

'I want out. It's over. I'm sorry,' I said.

'But you aren't saying anything. What's wrong? Did I do something to upset you?' she asked.

'I can't take it any more. I think that it's best that we break up,' I said.

'Take what?' She tried to understand. 'Is it because of Kimberley? That's my job, Tumi. What do you want me to do?' she asked.

At the time I was working as a TV producer for *180 Degrees*, the flagship current affairs programme for SABC Africa, the SABC's international TV channel, and she was working as a TV news reporter in Kimberley, so we were now in a long-distance relationship. I had been in one before and it did not work out very well. Because of my past experiences I was pessimistic about the future of our relationship, and that influenced how I engaged in this relationship. We fought over everything. We fought about the age gap between us, we fought about the respect levels in our relationship, we fought about our cultural differences and values. She accused me of having patriarchal tendencies, while I tried in vain to show her that the empowering of women does not necessarily mean the disempowering of men. We fought over inconsequential things like head-wraps, we fought about African spirituality versus Christianity, we fought about ancestors, we fought about the concept of lobola and we fought about gender roles. I felt that issues that could've been easily resolved were exacerbated by the distance between us. Everything was such a struggle. I wanted out.

My opportunity would come when she came back to Joburg for her birthday. She always wanted people around, and whenever she came to town I would drive her around to see family and friends. It was during one such run that one of her cousins mistakenly referred to me as Phuti, her ex-boyfriend. Phuti was the name that kept coming up in our relationship and I was now sick and tired of it. So, when I was accidentally referred to as Phuti, long after they had broken up, I was instantly defeated. It was not the main issue. It was a small issue, but one that became a tipping point.

'Let's just be friends,' I told her, after dropping her off at her mother's place.

'But how, when you're not telling me what I did wrong?' she asked.

I could not tell her about the name issue because I felt that she would think that I was being petty. I *was* being petty, but when emotions are high sometimes it's hard to think straight.

'It's for the best,' I said.

'OK, gaan met jou mince maar – Go with your nonsense then,' she said, deflated.

―

Shortly after the break-up I was offered a sponsored work trip to cover the plight of the Darfuri refugees who were living on the eastern fringes of Chad. I jumped at the opportunity. What better way to get over someone than to travel, I thought. I had been to Zambia before, and to the Democratic Republic of the Congo to report on the Congolese refugees.

This particular trip was organised by the Save Darfur Coalition, an advocacy group based in the United States. Its aim was to encourage African journalists to learn more about and report on the situation in Darfur and the suffering of the Darfuri people. A group of journalists from different African regions were to participate in a week-long media trip to eastern Chad, on the Darfur border, and to the surrounding refugee camps. At the time an indefinite but emphatically large number of people had been killed as a result of the Sudan and Darfur conflict, and more than 2.5 million people had been displaced. Over 200 000 Darfuri refugees were living in the refugee camps in Chad, and others in a network of camps in Darfur. Save Darfur covered all our costs and provided us with security, travel and health insurance. We would begin the trip in N'Djamena, the Chadian capital, and go on to Bahaï, Abéché, Goz Beïda and then Djabal.

Travelling abroad with a cameraperson can be complicated. The equipment (the cameras, lighting, tripod, cables and batteries) all has to be insured. A letter from the destination country's Ministry of Communications has to be secured before any kind of filming can happen. Most African countries have strict measures in place when it comes to television crews and filming. Government institutions are no-go areas, for example, so it's always advisable to first get clarity on what you may and may not film, lest you find yourself in a prison, like Chikurubi in Zimbabwe. But luckily for me and for my cameraperson, Japan Mathebula, the Chadian government assisted us just in time for the trip.

We arrived in Chad on 1 February 2008. But on the following day, in a surreal turn of events, Chadian rebel forces opposed to Chadian President Idriss Déby entered N'Djamena from Massaguet after a three-day advance through the country. Fortunately for us, by the time they entered the capital, we were in Bahaï. The rebels took a large part of the city and attacked the presidential palace. Telephone services and other communications were cut off throughout the country. We were in the middle of a coup d'état, on foreign soil. But I was not scared at all. At the time I didn't quite understand the gravity of what was happening. I was a young, naive journalist who was more excited about being caught up in a coup than worried about the possibility of losing my life. At first, I tried to do live telephonic interviews for SAfm and SABC Africa using a high-frequency walkie-talkie but I kept struggling to find reception.

'Japan, can we please shoot some mock crossings on the streets?' I asked my cameraperson, a scrawny and proud Zulu man with a broad smile.

I wanted to pre-record some stuff and feed it once we found the right facilities and had internet connectivity back.

'Chief, do you know that if you die here then your family will have to come all the way to Chad to fetch your spirit?' he said.

'Really?' I asked.

'And do you know that if they don't do that then your restless spirit will wander in limbo for all of eternity here in Chad?' he said with a serious face.

I laughed.

'Chief, I think it's best that you just keep your head down and stay with the rest of us,' he advised.

My excitement died down, and the real work that I was there for resumed. I was there to cover the story of the Darfuri refugees and not to get caught up in the internal politics of Chad.

―

Everyone back home was concerned about our safety, including Elrees, who contacted me via a mutual friend on Facebook. I was surprised but happy. There was something in the way she reached out to me that made me think that perhaps we were not really over, that maybe a couple more chapters of our story still needed to be written. A war-time environment does get one thinking a little differently about life and about one's choices and decisions, and I found myself thinking deeply about a possible future with Elrees. She didn't have to reach out to me, but she had. There was fight in her, and I liked it.

The rebels did not manage to capture the palace in the two days of fighting. They withdrew from the capital city and retreated to the east of the country. But for security reasons we still couldn't leave Chad via the capital. So the Save Darfur Coalition organised a light aircraft from Goz Beïda which flew us out safely to neighbouring Cameroon. From Cameroon we took connecting flights to Senegal and Kenya to drop off all the other journalists and then we flew back to South Africa. I was happy and relieved to be home.

A week later I went straight to Kimberley so Elrees and I could 'talk'. It was Friday. She fetched me from the bus stop. She smiled when she saw me, and gave me a long, close hug.
    'I'm so glad you guys made it out safely,' she said.
    'Thank you for reaching out to me,' I said.
    'You've lost some weight and your skin is a little darker.'
    'I know. It was a hectic experience. I'm glad it's over.'
    She was glowing. Kimberley was really treating her well, I thought.
    'Should we get some takeaways?' I asked.
    'No, don't worry, I prepared us something,' she said.
    We got into her bottle-green Nissan Sentra and headed

straight to her flat. At her flat we didn't do much talking. It was our bodies that did most of the talking. Nothing official was spoken but that night we were certainly official once more. In the morning our bodies did some more talking. We spent the afternoon actually talking about my experiences on the trip and about the troubles she was having at work. On Sunday evening I caught the last bus back to Joburg so I could be back in time for work on Monday.

My experience in Chad had left something stirring in me. I had interacted with a number of different people whose life experiences were completely different to mine. I spoke to 20-year-old Ameen Ibrahim, who was attacked in his village by the Janjaweed in 2006. They drove a knife deep into his eyes and left him for dead. Fortunately he survived, but he now lived a life where he was completely reliant on other people for help.

I spoke to Fazilah Mabior, who told me about how the Janjaweed took her from her village and kept her for three months as a sex slave until she fell pregnant. At the time she was kidnapped she was with her child, a baby boy. The Janjaweed killed the child in front of her. She then crossed the border and came to Chad, where she miscarried the baby she was carrying as a result of being raped repeatedly. I spoke to sisters Nafisa Hassan and Tabitha Hassan, who told me how their mother was murdered by the Janjaweed while they were planting millet with their father. They had just recently lost their father and were now left orphaned.

It was interactions like this that had me thinking differently about my life and what I wanted to do with it. I wanted to travel and to make a difference by telling more stories like these, or by doing work for organisations like the United Nations High Commissioner for Refugees and the International Red Cross.

One day I asked Elrees, via email, if she could wait for me. I did not want to lose her, but I also couldn't shake off this deep need to travel more and work on altruistic projects.

'What if I wait and it turns out to be just that, a promise? What if I wait and the promise is never fulfilled? What if I wait and time tells you that I'm not the one?' she emailed back. 'Pursue your dreams, Tumi. Don't let me hold you back. Do what makes you happy and don't apologise for it. I think it's best that we separate.'

'Let's have a baby?' I then offered, in haste, as insurance for our relationship, again by email. It was a terrible idea. I wanted to have it all. A loving woman back home waiting for me while I was up and about in the world doing Lord knows what. It was a completely ridiculous proposition. I am appalled at the thought now.

'As much as I am broody and love kids, I also want to know that I'm raising the kids with their father,' she politely declined. 'If I just wanted a kid I could go to the sperm bank. I want to share something beautiful and eternal with the father before the two of us consummate our union and bring into this world another being,' she wrote.

On 18 March 2008 she sent me another email to tell me that she could no longer go ahead with the relationship. 'You are my ideal mate in more ways than one, but the age thing really is an issue for me and I don't think we can downplay it any longer,' she said. I did not take her seriously.

A week later she missed her period. She took a home test and it confirmed that she was indeed pregnant.

'I'm pregnant,' she told me over the phone.

'Huh?'

'I'm going to be a mommy,' she said, with a smile in her voice.

'Should I come down?' I asked.

'No, don't worry. I need to go to the gynae first to confirm.'

'How are you feeling otherwise?'

'I'm fine, and you?'
'I don't know,' I said, still a little surprised by the news.
'I love you,' she said.
'I love you too,' I responded.

Talk of breaking up and of me wanting to travel across Africa fell by the wayside. I was going to be a father now. I was not scared at all when I heard the news. I was just surprised that I actually had it in me to make somebody pregnant. Up until that point I hadn't really thought deeply about my sperm as being this crucial component in the value chain of life creation, and now that it was, I was taken aback. Even though I knew about biology and the science of reproduction, I had never thought deeply about my sperm beyond the pleasurable, orgasmic feeling that I got whenever I discharged it.

It was not a planned pregnancy. Maybe it was, at a subconscious level, but at a conscious level Elrees and I did not sit down and discuss having a baby. We did not go out of our way to conceive. But maybe we did. Perhaps it was my subconscious way of trying to secure our relationship beyond my current need to travel and do meaningful work, and beyond the physical distance between us at the time. Normally Elrees would let me know when it was safe for me to come inside her and when it was not. This time, she had told me that she was not sure, because she had her cycle days mixed up, and normally when she was unsure I would pull out. But on this occasion I just couldn't do it. I honestly don't know whether I even tried to pull out or not. I don't know if the session was that pleasurable or if on some level I wanted to get her pregnant. I honestly do not know.

Even now, I wonder if I did not in fact trap her that night. I wonder if I took away her right to decide when exactly she wanted to fall pregnant, even though it was an open secret between us that she did want to have a baby. But was it truly my decision to make, whether I was actively conscious of it or not?

Or was it all in God's divine plan anyway, no matter what did that night? I wonder.

―

The first person I told about the news was my mother. Her initial response to the news was thoughtful rather than enthusiastic. Maybe she was not ready to be a gogo, or maybe she felt that I was still too young to be a father, even though I was now 26 years old. I think perhaps she was worried about how my life was going to change.

'How is Elrees doing there in Kimberley?' she asked.

'She's fine. The baby is fine,' I told her.

'I think you guys should name the baby Chad,' she suggested jokingly.

'No,' I said, unimpressed.

'How about naming the baby after me? Daisy Francina Dikeledi?' she said.

To which I replied with an emphatic 'Hell, naw!'

14

Great expectations

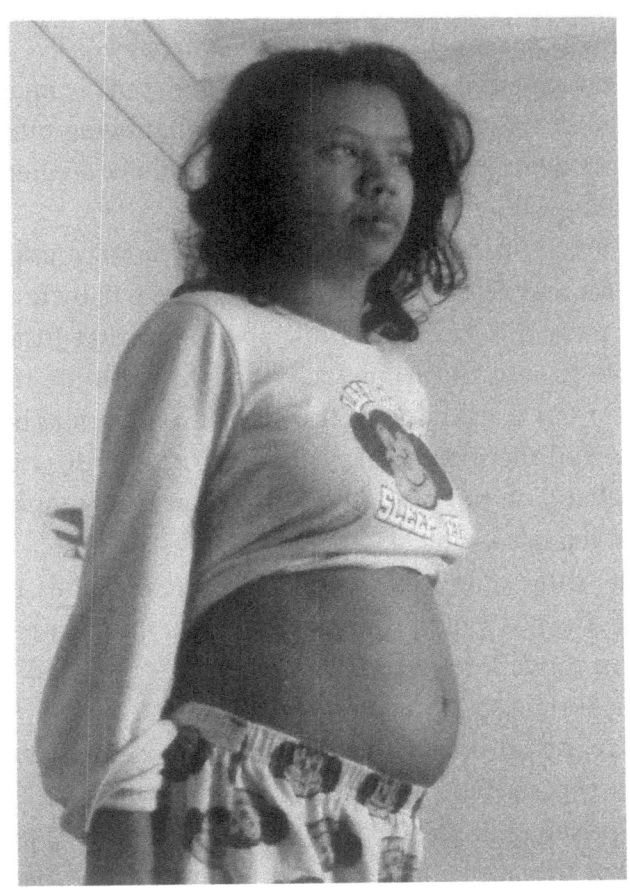

In the first few weeks of her pregnancy Elrees felt weak and sick most of the time, and all she wanted to do was sleep. On days when she was feeling a little better she would playfully ask if she could resign from her work and re-enter the job market only after all our babies had been born.

'Babies? How many babies is this woman planning on having?' I would ask myself.

Our phone and email conversations were mostly about how bad her nausea spells were. One day I told her that I was tired of talking about it all the time.

'Imagine how I must be feeling!' she snapped.

I had no experience dealing with a pregnant woman and we had plenty such fights. I was of the view that being pregnant did not give her licence to be rude and to act out. I wrote her an email to let her know how I felt.

'You have a lot of good qualities that I admire and that I'm thankful for and they certainly outweigh the bad by far,' I began. 'But you have this know-it-all air about you that just gets me. Really gets to me, and I must say that this attitude really does nothing for our conversations. I feel that you are just being condescending all the time. Rees, you don't know it all, your word is not gospel and on top of that you still refuse to humble yourself whenever you are wrong,' I wrote.

Exactly three minutes later she replied. 'Babe, I'm sorry, please forgive me. I didn't mean to rub you up the wrong way. I really have to work hard to let go of this "know-it-all" attitude. Please forgive me.'

I was really surprised that she responded immediately and that she accepted that she was wrong without protest. I was even more surprised that she actually used the words 'I'm sorry'. I figured that it was probably her hormones talking, because the Elrees that I knew would never just say sorry so effortlessly.

Towards the end of April I arranged a meeting with the elders of both families so I could formally accept *molato waka* - the wrong that I had committed against her. Normally the woman's family comes to the man's family to report the 'stomach' and to determine if the man accepts the responsibility of the 'stomach' or not. In our case there was really no need for any of this. We were both young, working adults and I had accepted that I was the father of the baby. So the meeting that I arranged was really more of a function to formally introduce the two families to each other.

I felt that my mother's house in Dunnottar was a better venue than my father's place. My father was never a people person, and I always got a sense from him that his place was off limits when it came to entertaining, so I didn't even bother to ask him.

Present at the meeting from my side of the family was myself, my mother, my father, my father's cousin-brother Uncle Ronnie and my mother's big brother Uncle Zakes. From Elrees' side of the family it was herself, her mother Gloria, her father Uncle John, her mother's sister Aunty Fanie and Fanie's husband Uncle Loemie. Elrees wore a long skirt with a shawl over her shoulders, and her hair was covered. She was the polar opposite of the cheeky shorts-wearing and sports-talking lassie that my father had met just a year ago. Her body language was contrite.

Uncle Zakes told her that it was unnecessary for her to carry herself in that way because we were not that kind of family. She laughed and loosened up a bit. We sat outside by the poolside, Elrees and I next to each other. The atmosphere was chatty, as if the two families had known each other for a long time. When the meeting officially commenced we were each asked about our plans and intentions. 'For now, I don't want to think too much about the future or be pressured into anything. Tumiso and I spoke and we agreed that we are having this baby together. So that's all for now,' said Elrees, holding my hand in a show of unity.

I nodded.

'But Elrees, it's not good for children to grow up outside of a marriage. I'm not saying rush into anything. But I'm saying think about the child,' said her mother, Gloria.

From the time we broke the news to her mother she was not too pleased at all.

'I'm not happy. That's why there's so many street kids out there today, because they come from broken homes. I'm really not happy,' she had told us, as dramatic as ever.

'Glo, the baby will be fine. Tumiso and I have agreed that for now we're just going to take it one step at a time,' said Elrees, a little annoyed.

Again I just nodded.

'The decision is ultimately yours,' said Uncle Zakes. 'You know, guys, when a kitten is small it's cute, adorable and lovely. But when it grows into a cat and its whiskers come out, then it isn't so appealing any more. You must always make sure that you have scissors in your hands to trim those whiskers every time they get out of hand,' he philosophised.

To this day I still don't understand what my Uncle Zakes was trying to say exactly.

Not one to be outdone, Elrees' father, Uncle John, probably also said something just as 'profound' to get a laugh out of everyone. But I just don't remember now. My father was good-humoured and kind throughout the meeting. I'd say that it was a successful meeting, even though Elrees' mother Gloria didn't quite get the outcome that she had been hoping for.

———

On 9 July 2008 Elrees sent me an email:

> I dreamt that the baby was born and it was very cute. It was a beautiful baby and it was wise beyond its years. In the dream I

wanted to breastfeed but the baby didn't want to latch on. [...] December now seems SO far away. I'm now beginning to feel REALLY EXCITED! I'M GONNA BE A MOMMA!

Excitement also came over me as I read the email. She was using the words 'baby' and 'it' because I did not want to know the sex of the baby. I had made her swear not to reveal it to me. She was in Kimberley and I was in Johannesburg, so I couldn't share much in the pregnancy. Not knowing and just imagining was my way of being a part of it. I wanted to find out only when the baby was born, just like in the olden days. But she could only keep this up for so long.

On Monday 15 July 2008 I called to check up on her. We hadn't spoken for the whole weekend.

'Hey what's up?' she answered.

'Nothing much. Just checking up on you. Or should I say on 'you guys'?' I said with a chuckle.

'We're good. I'm good. Baby is good. She's actually ...'

'Really Rees?' I exclaimed.

'I'm so sorry, I wasn't thinking!' she said.

'You always do this to me. You couldn't let me have this one thing. Just this one thing. I must go. We'll talk later,' I said.

'Tumiso, wait. I didn't mean for it to slip. Honestly,' she pleaded.

'Sure,' I said and then I hung up.

She called me back. I didn't answer. She called again. I still didn't answer.

I couldn't bring myself to talk to her. I wrote her an email instead in the afternoon, when I had calmed down and gathered my thoughts.

> I never thought I'd feel like this about such good news. It was really not your place to let it slip. You took something away

from me. Ignorance is bliss for a fool like me. I was really looking forward to the unknown, what God had in store for me, and I feel you took that away from me. Maybe you did do it intentionally. Just because you know now I must also know. But this was my way of feeling like I'm part of the pregnancy. My way of bonding with the baby. Possibilities in my head were wide and abounding. Now my excitement and anticipation is gone. Possibilities are limited and narrow. Honestly I'm not in the right headspace and I'm not thinking clearly. I just want to be left alone for a while. Whatever happens I will always be there for my daughter and I would love for her to be a Mashaba. I'd like us not to involve our family on this one and to try to sort it out between the two of us, if at all it can be sorted.

Reading this now I shudder at how melodramatic I was. One would think that I was the one who was pregnant from the way I was behaving.

Elrees responded the following morning:

I did not do it intentionally. God knows I didn't. It hurts that you're threatening to end the relationship because of a slip of the tongue on my part. I was bonding and chatting to her all weekend because I was by myself and by Monday when we spoke she was a real person to me, like she is now. She can be a Mashaba. I'd also love for her to have your surname. Involving families? Of course not, like you say, not at this stage.

If you want us to break up, that would hurt but I'll get over it. I'm just tired of you threatening to always leave when things are not going your way. This is life. There will be challenges and it will get very tough at times but for you to want to question the relationship at every turn is not fair. I will leave you alone for as long as you need, but please make a decision that you will stick to for life. In other words, do you want to be with ALL of me or just certain parts of me? Let me know what you decide. As far as bonding and being a part of the baby's life, that is something I will never deny you or your family.

I came around eventually. Begrudgingly. But I came around.

With the cat now out of the bag, I proudly announced on Facebook that I was going to be a father of a baby girl. Reboile, a close friend of mine at the time, wrote on my wall:

Hey Tumi, I am sooooooooo happy for you. You are going to enjoy fatherhood so much and you know I have always thought you will make a good dad. I have always believed that little girls hold a very special place in their hearts for their dads. She really is lucky to have you as a dad.

I was really moved by Reboile's words.

But I wonder what my reaction would've been if Elrees had said 'he' instead of 'she'. I doubt that I would have been so melodramatic. At first I blamed it on the jitters that come with being a soon-to-be-dad. I rationalised my reaction as nothing more than the anxiety that usually comes with a pregnancy. But when I think about it now, it was really because my hopes had been dashed on some subliminal level. I think that deep down I was expecting a boy. Even though I did not want to know the sex of the baby, I was hoping for a boy. It's not an easy thing to admit to oneself, but I think that my unreasonable reaction really stemmed from disappointment.

15

Synové
(A gift from the sun)

SYNOVÉ (A GIFT FROM THE SUN)

On 20 September 2008, as Elrees was getting ready for work, she felt a sharp pain in her stomach. 'I don't think I'm going in to work today. I think there's something wrong,' she told me over the phone, in a panic.

'Is it the baby?' I asked.

'I don't know. But I have this really sharp pain in my stomach, and I can barely move,' she said.

I tried to reassure her. She told me she would call the doctor and let me know what was happening later.

Around 15:00, an hour from knock-off time, she gave me a ring. She sounded a lot calmer.

'It's a urinary tract infection. The doctor is keeping me overnight for some more observations. But you should make your way down here because apparently the baby might come at any moment,' she said.

An average pregnancy lasts for 38 weeks or nine months from the date of conception. Elrees was in the middle of her second trimester. At this stage the baby's organs had fully formed, and her hearing was now well developed. Her face looked like a newborn's, though her cheeks were yet to fill, her skin was still wrinkled and thin, and her body was now well-muscled and almost proportionate to her head, though still thin.

But it was still not a good sign at all, even though the survival rate of infants in the second trimester is usually between 60 and 70 per cent. The situation was hanging in the balance. Things could still go either way. For Elrees and for the baby.

But after the phone call I was overcome by excitement. I couldn't wait to finally say that I was someone's father. I couldn't wait for the applause, the congratulations and the recognition that come with bringing a life into this world. All I heard from that phone call was that the baby was coming – not might come, but was coming – and in my boastful excitement I immediately posted something on Facebook.

At that stage in my life, I was actually more concerned with the flood of adoring reactions that I was likely to receive from sharing the news on Facebook than I was with the potential complications that can arise from a premature delivery. So, I wonder, was I really ready to be a father?

I left for Kimberley that very day.

On 21 July Elrees had written to her work informing them that her doctor was recommending that her workload be reduced. She would not be able to work every second weekend. This was because she had a low-lying placenta, which meant that she was more susceptible to a urinary tract infection, which could result in premature labour. She told them that July would be her last month on the weekend roster, because her doctor had recommended that she work only one weekend a month. She also told them that she was going to be off on Monday and Tuesday, in compensation for the previous weekend that she had worked, and that she would be taking Wednesday off for her antenatal appointment.

On 31 July her managers emailed her the roster for August. They had her down for a shift every second weekend. When she queried this, she was told that she had to submit a sick note as proof that she had consulted with a doctor on a Friday back in February when she had left work without permission. She also had to supply a medical report with the recommendations from her gynaecologist, and this would be used to kick-start the process of sending her for a second medical opinion. Elrees made sure that all the requested documents were submitted.

Her work problems were not new. They had started at the beginning of the year, when she first called for an overtime system to be implemented. She felt that the long and irregular hours the journalists were working were not being properly compensated

SYNOVÉ (A GIFT FROM THE SUN)

for. This didn't go down well with management.

As a result of this, and a series of unrelated events that happened in a space of less than two months, she was served with disciplinary papers alleging insubordination. She was charged with cancelling a satellite feed booking without permission for a story that she felt was nothing more than a PR exercise; for changing a story angle while she was in the field; and for not being able to find a story, any story, that could be included in the diary.

Elrees dismissed the charges as trumped up. To me they were indeed a clear indication that the managers were gunning for the 'loudmouth' in the office more than anything. At the time I did not understand – and I still do not understand to some extent – the complex nature of the victimisation that many women have to contend with at work. Instead, I felt that she was putting her ego first by taking on her superiors while she was pregnant with our baby. She, in turn, felt that I was being chauvinistic and uncaring towards her plight, and that I was taking the side of her bosses, who had no sympathy for a pregnant woman. In truth she was fighting for her rights.

At the time she was also alone in Kimberley while her family was back in Joburg, stressed not only about her job, but about the health of our baby too.

The disciplinary hearing was postponed on three occasions for various reasons. It finally convened on 14 August. Elrees, in her second trimester, would sit in these hearings for a total of 18 hours.

Because I had left Joburg in such a rush I hadn't filled in a leave application. But my manager at work was a very understanding man. When I called him he said, 'No problem,' and wished me well.

A FATHER IS BORN

The following morning Elrees was given antibiotics and discharged from hospital. Her gynaecologist in Kimberley was sceptical about doing the delivery prematurely, so she sent Elrees home and gave her two weeks off work.

'I'm worried,' Elrees told me back at her flat.

'It will be fine,' I told her, trying to be positive.

The following day Elrees was in pain again.

'The baby can't stop moving,' she told me. I wasted no time in taking her back to the hospital where we were told she needed an emergency delivery. It was touch and go, and we couldn't waste any more time. Elrees was immediately prepped for theatre.

'Please call our folks and let them know what's happening,' she asked me. I did. I also went to my car to fetch my video camera.

Elrees was very anxious. I tried to cheer her up by making jokes. But she was preoccupied. She had hoped to have the baby in Joburg, with her family around. She had also hoped that her Johannesburg-based gynaecologist would be the one who did the delivery.

As they wheeled her to theatre I began recording with my video camera. I pressed 'pause' as the door slid open to allow us in. Inside, one of the attending nurses gave me a hairnet and scrubs to put on. The anesthetist injected Elrees' lower back with an epidural.

Elrees took my hand and said, 'Let's pray.'

As she was praying, I thought of how best to break the news on Facebook. When she finished her prayer I resumed recording, making sure that I didn't miss anything.

'Maybe I can post some of this footage,' I thought. I was present and yet not fully present in the moment. I was actually employing a journalistic technique, where one suspends emotions so it is easier to impartially record unfolding events, blow by blow. I was treating the birth of my firstborn child as a news story and I was not even aware of it.

The doctors cut Elrees open just above her pubic area. The baby was blueish when they yanked her out. She didn't cry out loud as I knew most babies do. All her limbs, fingers and toes were fully developed. But she was frail and thin, a tiny little figure. The paediatrician placed her on a small table and pressed against her chest with the tips of her fingers. She gave her oxygen through a small nozzle which she taped in place to keep it from moving. She said that the baby had ingested too much water into her lungs while she was still in Elrees' stomach, and she was struggling to breath.

After a while, she managed to stabilise the baby and get her to breathe through an oxygen ventilator. Our newborn baby was to be kept in ICU for a long while, it seemed. But I was relieved

Elrees was weak, in pain and a little out of it from the medication.

At that point I phoned everybody about the arrival of baby, Synové Lerothodi Mashaba. They were all pleased.

'Don't forget to get today's newspapers,' my mother told me.

'Why?' I asked.

'So you can show them to Synové when she is big, and she can read about what happened in the world on the day she was born,' she said.

'Or she can just read it online,' I said, trying to be a smart-ass.

'It's not the same,' she said.

'Yes, I know. I will get the newspapers,' I said. I never did.

―――

I spent the greater part of the following day at the hospital, looking after Elrees and taking videos and pictures of our newborn baby. But our newborn baby wasn't looking too good at all. There were all these tubes coming in and out of her, and she had on the smallest of nappies, which looked oversized on her scrawny body. Neither of us could hold her. All we could do was look at her through the glass partition. I was emotionally and physically exhausted. Elrees was just as burnt out, but she was very happy that Synové was alive. She was hopeful that now that Synové was out of her stomach she would make it through.

When I left the hospital in the afternoon the first thing I did was get myself a six-pack of beer and some takeaway food. I had reached a great milestone in my life. I was now a father. But I couldn't fully enjoy the moment. I had no appetite to update anyone on Facebook on the developments. I thought about how, culturally, it is not considered advisable for one to share news around a pregnancy prematurely. It is believed that such news should be closely guarded until the last trimester at least. It is believed that we curse the pregnancy when we announce it prematurely to just about anyone, because not everyone is pleased and happy for you, and that spirit of bitterness alone is enough to cause great harm. I thought about this that night and I deeply regretted being seduced by the allure of social media. I slept uneasily that night.

In the morning I was woken up early by a phone call from Elrees.

'You need to get here as soon as possible,' she said.

'What's happening?' I asked, wiping the sleep off my face with my hand.

'It's bad,' she told me. 'Just get here.'

When I got to the hospital Synové's vital signs were dropping drastically. The nurses and the doctor were trying their best to resuscitate her. But her signs just kept dropping and dropping. Elrees held my hand and prayed, loudly and fearlessly. She begged God to spare Synové's life.

The attending doctor turned to us.

'There's nothing more I can do for her. There's too much water in her lungs and she has developed an infection that is becoming harder and harder to treat,' she said.

We watched as her vital signs dropped, until the line was completely flat and there was no more life left in her.

'I'm so sorry,' said the doctor before she left.

Elrees let out a devastated wail. I held her tight as she cried bitterly. The nurses switched off the machines and took out all the tubes that were coming in and out of our baby's body. 'Do you want to hold her and say goodbye?' one of the nurses asked Elrees. She nodded, her eyes puffy and teary. She settled herself gently on the bed and held on tight. She spoke to Synové, pleadingly, begging her to come back. But she was gone, and Elrees gave the baby back to the nurse.

We were told that her cause of death was respiratory distress syndrome. Babies born at a very premature stage may have lungs that are so stiff that they cannot breathe on their own, and when they are able to start breathing the lungs may collapse because of insufficient air. The doctors said this was the case with our baby.

In the afternoon Elrees was discharged from hospital.

———

When we arrived at her flat she went straight to the bathroom. She closed the door and cried. I, in front of the door, dropped to the floor and I cried as well. We stayed like that for about an hour, each of us in our own separate spaces. She came out to get a fresh pad from her toiletry bag and a bucket from the kitchen.

She was walking slowly, in extreme physical pain from the caesarean stitches just above her pubic area.

'Can you please help me with this bucket? I need to relieve myself,' she asked.

'Sure,' I said.

She found it difficult to use the toilet in her current state. When she used the bucket a huge amount of afterbirth discharge and blood came out. It was messy.

'I'm so sorry. This is so embarrassing,' she said.

'Don't worry about it,' I reassured her. I held the bucket until she was finished and then cleaned up and helped her to change her dressing. She was absolutely shattered.

'Is God punishing me? Why is this happening? She was a real person to me. My baby. Why did this happen? Why? I want my baby back. Please Lord, I want her back. I want my baby back. I want my baby back,' she went on and on and cried some more.

That night I received a text message from my father simply saying, 'I'm sorry.' My mother and her boyfriend Nic, who now ran a funeral parlour, drove to Kimberley to fetch the body from the hospital that night. My mother had expected to come to Kimberley with new baby clothes. But now she was coming to fetch the body of her firstborn grandchild. It was a devastating blow to her.

In the morning we drove back to Johannesburg ahead of the funeral. Just a week earlier I had been on top of the world, posting statuses on Facebook about being a soon-to-be-dad. Now I was driving back to bury my firstborn child. I had been looking forward to spending many, many days and nights with her, laughing and playing together until the end of time. But Synové, it seems, was just a sprinkle, a taste, a tickle and a droplet, just as I had named her – Lerothodi – and just like that she was gone from my life. What cut up Elrees even more was that during the funeral and the burial service she kept producing milk. The tablets they had given her to stop lactating hadn't kicked in yet.

16

Picking up the pieces
Part 2

Losing Synové felt surreal to me at first. Like it wasn't happening. Like I was just dreaming. But it was real and it was happening. It happened. I was not dreaming at all. That all-too-familiar sunken feeling came over me. It felt like my whole life was just a long, laborious process of trying to get right what could never be. I felt like it was just one big futile exercise with no real meaning to it, a constant struggle.

I accepted, bitterly, that loss was a part of my being and of my history which would remain forever tragically intertwined with my future. I felt like whatever I built, whatever I loved, whatever I nurtured was and would always be taken away from me. That the promise of growth and fullness would always exist. But that that promise would never get to bloom.

Is it possible for any one person to grieve for their entire life? At that point I felt as if I had been grieving forever. I was overwhelmed by emotions. I found it difficult to eat and sleep. During that period I consumed more alcohol than I've ever done before or since. I questioned my life, my choices and my purpose on this earth, and I did not get any satisfactory answers. Even though I kept myself clean because I had to go to work every day, I did not have the energy to tidy my place up. I lived in a pile of dirty dishes and dirty clothes.

They say grieving is a natural response to loss. That we all go through it at some point. It's necessary for our healing. That grieving is a force for change in our lives because it brings us to a deeper understanding of life, and the more significant the loss the more intense the grieving process. But it's not a pleasant experience. It takes time, it cannot be forced, it cannot be hurried and there's still no guarantee of healing at the end of the process. It's a messy, jumbled-up affair taking one from denial to anger, bargaining, depression and acceptance. And you can still end up where you started.

Some say there is no right or wrong way to grieve because

grieving is an individual experience. And they say that people can do the most unthinkable of things. I was no exception.

Less than a month after losing Synové I started seeing Lerato, a work colleague of mine who sat across from me. Lerato was a short, dreadlocked, light-skinned and cute-faced young lady who I had become close friends with over the last couple of months. I'd say our friendship started in more or less the same way as my friendship with Elrees. Lerato had found out that I had access to the SABC's recorded music library, and there were some CDs that she wanted to get her hands on, so I obliged. We liked the same kind of music. We were both huge fans of the Soulquarians collective – artists like Erykah Badu, D'Angelo, The Roots and Common. We both loved A Tribe Called Quest with a passion. We were both sneaker-heads. We shared similar ideas on what an ideal relationship should look like. We were both averse to the idea of marriage and of being 'chained down' to someone for all of eternity. We were leaning more towards the idea of a life partner in our thinking. I saw so much of myself in her.

With Elrees being away in Kimberley, the situation gave room for us to develop a friendship that was to become dangerous, especially for a man who was in a long-distance and committed relationship. When it began, Lerato knew that I was in a serious relationship and was expecting a child. She too was in some kind of long-term relationship. At that point I didn't see anything untoward about our friendship. She was a cool person that I liked to hang out with. Because she sat across from me in the office she would listen in to my telephone conversations with Elrees, and then she would give her unsolicited, two-cents worth of thoughts on the goings-on in my relationship. This used to seriously annoy me in the beginning.

'This place isn't exactly big enough for one to hold a private conversation, is it?' she once said when I raised the issue with her. But as time went on I found her to be a good sounding board.

Our conversations were easy and free-flowing. 'Like fish to water,' she used to say. We would be so engrossed in our talking that at times it felt as if we were the only two people in that office. She was one of only a handful of people there who knew that Elrees was expecting our first child. I also told her that I was planning on remaining the same person as I was, even after the baby arrived.

'You say that now, but the only thing that is constant in life is change. Things will change, mate, more so when your baby mama moves back this side,' she said.

'But why should things change? I think that's where people get it wrong – suddenly changing who they are when they have a baby or when they get married,' I said.

'You might find that when the little one arrives all the changes that you are fighting right now will happen automatically, without you even being aware of it. Like hanging out *le majita*, with the guys, on weekends, for example. You might find that you actually prefer staying at home with your family,' she said.

'Are you planning on being there for the birth?' she asked.

'Of course I am. I wouldn't miss it for the world,' I said.

We spoke about anything and everything. No subject was off limits. Once she told me that she wanted to visit a sex shop.

'Why?' I asked, with piqued interest.

'I'm curious,' she smiled.

'Why don't you go then?' I asked.

'I don't want to go on my own. You can come with me,' she offered, with a flirtatious smile.

I said nothing.

'Come on, I'm sure you've been dozens of times. You guys like this kind of stuff,' she said.

'Yeah, we do. But you are a girl,' I said, a little shy.

'So what? she said.

'So maybe it's not your kind of thing.'

'Maybe it is and maybe it isn't.'

'What do you want to get there anyway?' I asked.

'I don't know. Stuff. Some sex toys and DVDs maybe' she said.

I told her I would go with her, and I'd let her know when. We never got around to it. I figured that things were probably not going well in her relationship.

On another occasion I told her about my difficult past relationships and about how I found myself unable to stay faithful for a long time. I told her how I would stray whenever things got too serious.

'I'm really trying to give it my all this time around. It's not easy, especially with the distance, but I'm trying to be a better man,' I told her.

She didn't seem convinced at all. 'I don't see your straying days being over, and that worries me for her sake. She seems more invested in this than you,' she said.

I don't know if she planted the seed or simply watered the garden, but when she said 'I don't see your straying days being over' it rattled something inside me. It was just an opinion but there was some truth in it. It was as if she could see right through me. It was as if she knew who I really was at the core of my being and I disliked her for that. Even though she was right, albeit partially, it was still not her place to hold up a mirror to me. So for the next few months I cut ties with her and focused my energy back on my relationship with Elrees, and on our plans for our unborn baby.

When I came back to the office after Synové's passing, Lerato reached out to me. It had been a while since we had last spoken. She was kind and sincere. We then started reconnecting again. 'Like fish to water,' she reminded me.

Some weeks later she sent me an email recounting a wild sex dream that she'd had about me that had her all conflicted. I was surprised. But most of all I was flattered. I was mourning, yes. But

I was flattered all the same. It had been a while since Elrees and I had been intimate and I guess I was easy to bait. When I bumped into her after the email, she couldn't maintain eye contact. She was short, and as short as I was, I towered over her as we spoke. She looked sweet and vulnerable. I could see that she was embarrassed but I was moved by how open and honest she had allowed herself to be with me. It was risky for her to send me such an email that exposed the desires that lurked in her subconscious and I was hooked.

Her vulnerability had a magnetic pull. I was in a vulnerable place myself and I felt that maybe this was somebody that I could be one hundred per cent honest and true with. She wanted me and I wanted her.

'Can I come to your place tonight so we can talk some more about that email?' I asked her.

She nodded with a smile.

Now would a non-grieving Tumiso have entertained thoughts of another woman like that? Maybe yes and maybe no. It all depends on how long Tumiso has been grieving, and how long he has been conscious of his grieving. Has it been a month? Or has it been years now, without him even realising it? And still with no healing?

How one grieves is very important to the process. Some ways are healthy and ultimately helpful, and some ways are destructive. Was I trying to get out of a long-distance relationship that now seemed to serve no purpose by finding comfort between the sheets of another woman's bed? Was this what my father had been going through when he lost Tshepo? Was finding comfort in the arms of another woman his way of grieving? And was it helpful? Certainly not.

I felt no remorse for what I was doing. I was lost, a castaway from a shipwreck who had just proven to Lerato that his straying days were indeed far from over. I was going through my own process, I guess, no matter how flawed and destructive that process was.

Elrees was very bitter and angry at that time. The disciplinary committee hearing had found her guilty on only one of the charges, which was cancelling a feed without her manager's consent, and she got a written warning for it. She appealed, on the basis that it was for a story that she had disowned and therefore the issue of the cancellation of the feed was irrelevant. She believed that she was not guilty of insubordination because she had refused what she considered to be an unlawful instruction. But the unlawful instruction that she was referring to was not the same instruction that was cited in the report. According to Elrees, the unlawful instruction related to an instruction to sign off on a story which did not resemble the original that she had scripted. The internal appeals process took longer because of this confusion.

Elrees ended up taking the matter to the Commission for Conciliation, Mediation and Arbitration, the CCMA. She blamed the entire management team for what had happened. She was bitter and she was hurting. She wanted justice. She obsessed over the matter, and this, coupled with the distance between us, affected our relationship. I wanted out and my actions showed it. But I could not just break up. We had just lost a baby, which counted beyond everything. So, I lied. I played along.

Elrees came to visit one weekend. She was still healing from her caesarean. We hadn't been intimate for a while now. She wanted us to use condoms. But first she wanted me to get something from the pharmacy for her recurring urinary tract infection. She suspected that I was the one who kept re-infecting her because I was still uncircumcised at the time.

'There might be some bacteria or STDs under your foreskin that you may not be aware of,' she told me. She was probably right. While she had only me as a sexual partner, I was sexually active with other people. Sometimes I used protection and sometimes I didn't. She said that I must ask the pharmacist to prescribe something for me as well. I did.

When I came back from the shops I took a bath. Five minutes later, she walked into the bathroom with my phone in her hand and asked me who Lerato was. I was immediately furious. I went on the usual 'Why are you going through my phone?' and 'Why are you reading my messages?' rant. She asked me again who Lerato was. She had read all the flirty, booty call messages, and there was no denying what was right before her eyes. I was caught out. *Why did I not just delete these messages*, I thought. But that's what living alone does to you. You become sloppy and complacent about hiding your tracks. I told her that she was just a colleague and that we had kissed once, that's all. She didn't buy any of it.

'Not even two months have passed since our baby died, and you're busy with colleagues,' she said in disbelief. 'There's no more "us". We are over.'

She went to the bedroom and started packing her stuff. She asked me to take her home. On our way I kept apologising to her, but she was just quiet. I also fell quiet after a while. *It's just as well*, I thought, *since I want out of the relationship in any case*. My behaviour was definitely not that of someone who wanted to make the relationship work. I think that subconsciously I blamed Kimberley and her fights with her work for the messy state of our relationship. I was 26 years old and I felt like this relationship was fast eroding my prime years. If she had been around and not in Kimberley fighting her losing battles, then I wouldn't have cheated on her, I convinced myself.

When we got to her mother's place I parked outside, and then she offloaded on me.

'You know, Tumi, I was the one who carried the baby. I was the one that had bonded with her. I was the one who was going through the most hell. And then here you are being an asshole with another woman at work. It's not even two months since our baby died. How heartless can you be? You hurt me very much,' she said. 'I don't trust you any more and if you still want this relationship then I need you to work extra hard on regaining my trust again.'

Even though she was hurting and deeply disappointed, I could tell that she was not ready to let go.

'I will work harder on the relationship and I will put in more effort to regain your trust,' I told her. It was not the complete truth. I felt sorry for her. But more than anything, I felt guilty.

I stopped my dalliances with Lerato. But her invisible presence in our relationship would remain with us for some time to come. Neither was I suddenly cured after we had had our talk outside Elrees' mother's house. I was still a broken man who had tendencies to stray, whether actively or otherwise. I was still my father's child at the core of my being.

———

At the end of January or beginning of February in the New Year, Elrees came to pay me a visit. She did not have any bus fare, but she still wanted to see me. I could not quite understand the urgency of this trip. She came overnight by train, all the way from Kimberley, and I had to fetch her from Park Station in the early hours of the morning. The first thing that we did when we got back to my place was to make love on the couch. We fell asleep, right there on the couch. In the afternoon I drove her back to her mother's place.

The following month she arranged an intimate evening meeting with me at a restaurant at the Cresta Mall in Johannesburg. I had had it with our long-distance arrangement, and I wanted to break up with her. I felt it was the right thing to do. There was nothing else tying me to her and I felt she deserved better. I thought that this was the perfect opportunity to make a clean break.

When I got to the restaurant, she was looking amazing. She had her hair done in a bob and wore trendy denim dungarees. I was floored and I immediately reconsidered my decision to break up with her. After the small talk, she told me that she was pregnant.

'I would understand if you don't want to be with me any more, but I would love it if you could be a part of the baby's life,' she said.

I wondered if she had intuited that I was planning on breaking up with her. Women have a sixth sense about these things.

'When do you think this happened?' I asked, taken aback.

'On the morning when I came by train,' she said.

We laughed. I moved close to her. We hugged and kissed.

'I guess I'll have to start making plans to send my uncles to your family then,' I said. To this day I still maintain that that was my proposal of marriage to her in a roundabout way. I know it's not romantic. But in my culture, when a man says he is going to 'send his uncles', then he means business.

———

I think Elrees, in her grief, wanted to have another baby no matter what it took, even if it meant riding on a train overnight for more than eight hours to make it happen. I think that she was blinded by her grief, just as I had been misdirected by mine. Grief does have the power to make people do strange things. I was clearly not the right guy for her at the time. I had cheated on her and at the worst possible time. I was clearly not ready to be a father. How can I have been, if I was capable of behaving in that fashion? I had the propensity to be a big-time philandering loser.

All the signs were there, and she knew this, but she still got on that train to Joburg. With one mission in mind. To fall pregnant, even though she won't readily admit to it. And I, still burdened by my guilt, gave her what she most desired. Again, we did not sit down and discuss if we wanted to fall pregnant or not. It just happened. Maybe on a subconscious level we did want to have a baby. I don't know.

17

Imani
(Faith)

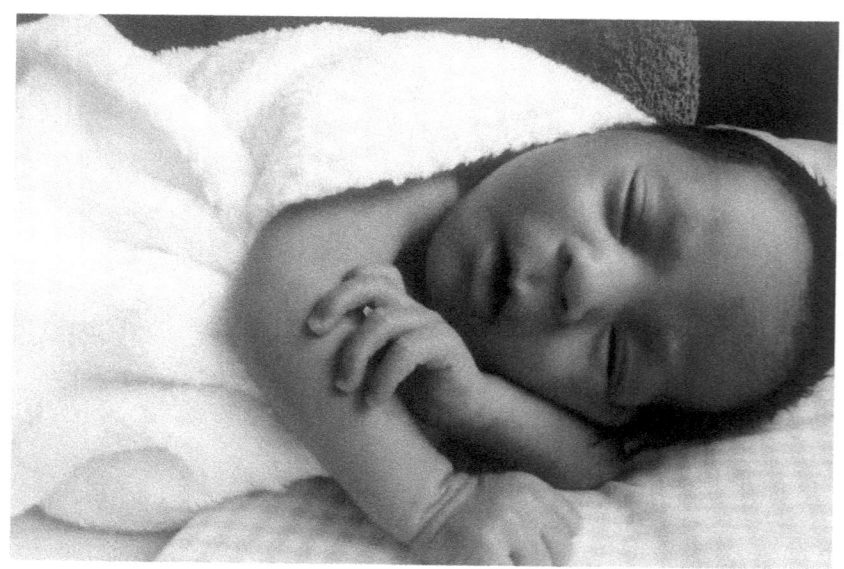

Elrees and I made a pact that we were going to keep this pregnancy a secret for as long as possible, and there would be no more premature social media status updates from my side either. We were wary of telling people because of what had happened to Synové. So, we kept the news to ourselves.

At the time I was having difficulty keeping up with the interest rates on my home loan and on the car I was driving – they had hiked as a result of the 2008 global economic meltdown. I had a baby on the way and needed to make an honest woman of Elrees. As a Christian woman it was absolutely scandalous for her to be having yet another baby out of wedlock, so she pushed for us to get married as soon as possible. She was worried about what her mother would say if she found out that she was pregnant again. So, she suggested that we go to Home Affairs to get it over with quickly.

'OK, but let me talk to my parents first,' I said.

I started by speaking to my mother. She advised that I should save up and structure my finances better before I considered getting married. She could sense that something was amiss, and she told me that she would not support us going to Home Affairs to get married there.

'I can lend you some money if you need, but I strongly recommend that you do things the proper way,' she stressed.

When I spoke to my father he told me more or less the same thing.

'In the history of the Mashaba family, no one has ever gone to Home Affairs to sign on their own. You just don't marry without the involvement of the families,' he told me. 'We just don't do that in this family. We gather first as a family and then you tell us of your intentions. Then we send a letter to the woman's family requesting a meeting. They then revert back to us with a suitable date and time for the meeting. Once we have received that information then a small party of your uncles goes over to the woman's family on the set date at the arranged time to ask for *'sego sa metsi'* – a bride – on your behalf.'

He continued to break it down: in the meeting the woman's family would set forth the expectations that I would have to meet before they could grant me their daughter's hand in marriage. The two families would go back and forth until they reached an amicable position. My uncles would then phone me to inform me of the terms set out by the woman's family, and they would ask me if I agree to the terms.

'If you agree, then they will leave behind the first portion of *magadi* or lobola that the family is expecting. They will then come back at a later stage to settle the balance, and at that point the two families will then agree that you can take your bride. Once that process is completed, then you and Elrees can decide if you want to go to Home Affairs so that the union can be officially recognised as a civil union, or if you want to get married in a church. It's up to you. That's how we do things, son.'

'But Elrees is coloured, and they do things differently,' I told him.

'It doesn't matter. This is how we do things and that's not negotiable,' he told me, not mincing his words.

―

Elrees was rather disappointed when I delivered the news to her. She told me that she was a Christian and she didn't want a traditional ceremony where she would be introduced to the ancestors and so on. I told her that I came from a very progressive family where she would not be forced to do anything she didn't want to do, but signing at Home Affairs without a proper union of the families was simply out of the question. Reluctantly she came around to my view. I then went back to speak to my mother and my father so we could set things in motion for the *magadi* negotiations. As promised, my mother loaned me some money towards the 'bridewealth'; the blankets for gifts, as a symbolic gesture of comfort to the woman's family because their daughter is leaving their home to start her own family; and the bottles of whisky and brandy to open the talks or to break the ice between the two families.

Elrees' family insisted that they did not want *magadi* because it was not a part of their culture, but we asked them to indulge us because of how we did things. They agreed.

But in the weeks before Elrees' family could meet ours to officially accept *magadi* in return for their daughter's hand in marriage, Elrees felt debilitating pangs just below her stomach. The pain was so severe that she could barely move. She said it felt like someone was driving a knife deep into her stomach. She tried to soldier on, but when it grew worse I had no choice but to rush her to the hospital. We were both worried about the baby, but we couldn't tell anybody in the family that we were expecting. At the hospital, they confirmed that there was nothing wrong with the baby. But they did find a massive kidney stone. They also discovered that she only had one kidney.

'Some people are born that way,' said the doctor. Elrees was put on a drip and they gave her some pain relief medication. When her mother came to the hospital we told her about the pregnancy.

'But please keep it to yourself for now,' we insisted.

Elrees was kept overnight. The following day they told her that the stone had been caused by a build-up of calcium in her urine. Since she only had one kidney, it was working overtime to help flush out all the toxins from her system. They told her it was caused by eating a diet that was high in salt. Normally they would just have given her medication to help break down the kidney stone, which she would then urinate out in small particles. But her kidney stone was big, and she was pregnant, and they did not want to strain her one and only kidney or place any unnecessary complication on the pregnancy. So they told her that they would put a ureteral stent, a thin hollow tube, in her ureter instead, to help her pass urine from the kidney into her bladder. This was a safer and a less invasive procedure for a pregnant woman. They told her that they could only remove the kidney stone laparoscopically after the pregnancy. After the stent insertion procedure, she was sent home.

I thought of cancelling the *magadi* talks, which had already been planned for the next weekend. My mother said we don't cancel such things.

'It's bad luck to cancel things like weddings once a date has been set and invitations sent out. Traditionally such things must go on no matter what,' she told me. 'Hurdles like this always happen when two families are being joined together. Something always goes wrong. Cars break down, the weather turns, the food goes off and at worst even death occurs. But the marriage must go on as agreed,' she stressed.

So, we settled on having a scaled-down affair instead, where it was just going to be the aunts and the uncles who were needed for the marriage talks and maybe a few of my friends and hers. After that conversation I pondered on why things always went wrong when two families were being joined together. I settled on it being a case of the ancestors from the two respective families not quite agreeing with each other on certain issues, with one side being just as stubborn as the other.

On 28 April 2009, a small party of my uncles and aunts, led by my father's cousin-brother Uncle Ronnie and my mother's older brother Uncle Zakes, left for the West Rand in the morning to officially ask on my behalf for *sego sa metsi* – my bride. The translation is beautiful – a gourd or calabash of water – symbolising life, which in turn symbolises a bride. They were

IMANI (FAITH)

going there to pay *magadi*, to exchange the gifts and to come back with my *makoti*, my bride, all in the same day. It was an unusual affair indeed and one that broke with tradition. As I mentioned before, Elrees' family didn't believe in, or want to participate in, the *magadi* process – they were merely indulging us. But it was a necessary step on our side, because one cannot simply take a *makoti* for *mahala* – for nothing. In our culture a *makoti* is a valuable asset that helps a man to build and expand his family and home. It's not child's play to take a *makoti*. So, the steps one takes when asking for a woman's hand in marriage are important in showing how serious a man is. He must be able to demonstrate to the woman's family that he can take care of her, and if he fails to come up with a reasonable bridewealth or offering to the woman's family, how can he possibly look after her?

Even though, traditionally speaking, I was not allowed to be present, I nevertheless accompanied the small party so I could show them the way to Elrees' home. But I could at least wait outside with my best friend, Mdeva, while the two parties met inside for the negotiations, engagement and marriage talks, all wrapped into one. The discussions, although cordial, were not easy at all, I'm told. The main bone of contention was the slaughtering part of the traditional ceremony. Elrees' mother, Gloria, was completely against the idea of slaughtering and of calling upon the ancestors at the traditional wedding we were planning on having.

'There isn't anything wrong with slaughtering, because even the meat that is sold in the butcheries is from slaughtered cattle,' Uncle Zakes argued, trying to convince her.

'It's not so much the slaughtering but the introduction of Elrees to the ancestors as a new *makoti* to the family that I have a problem with. As Christians we don't believe in that,' said Gloria.

'The introduction of Elrees to the ancestors doesn't necessarily equate to her now believing in them. It's purely an exercise of acknowledging them and informing them of the new developments in the land of the living. People like Abraham, Jacob and Isaac in the Bible also acknowledged their ancestors, by the way,' said Uncle Zakes.

But Gloria was not willing to move, and I'm told that in the end a compromise was reached where they agreed that that part of the traditional ceremony, should we decide to have one, would be left out. After the talks, the *magadi* money was presented on the table and counted by both sides of the family to make sure that it was the right amount. Afterwards it was agreed by both families that from that day onwards Elrees and I could live together as husband and wife. My side of the family then presented the gift blankets to her family, and we were treated to a delicious lunch. There was a jolly and warm atmosphere.

Elrees and I were now officially man and wife. But she didn't quite feel like someone's wife yet. In her mind, what constituted a union was a priest presiding over the marriage, with her in a white gown. That was her frame of reference. I did my best to try to convince her that the white wedding theatrics were really a celebration and not a marriage as such. In her mind what had transpired was an engagement. But in our culture we do not have such a thing as an engagement.

'A marriage is what took place today. When two families come together and agree that indeed their children should be joined in marriage. That is a marriage. What we are planning on having later on is a wedding, a celebration,' I told her. 'You can take comfort in the fact that we are no longer living in sin.'

But she was still not convinced. A white wedding and all the pomp and ceremony that came with it was the only thing that was going to convince her. I suppose she was right to be sceptical, given the objectionable nature of the way in which customary unions are generally treated in this country. But our legal system has since made some significant and progressive strides towards the full recognition of such unions. So I relented, and I promised her that we would have a white wedding after the birth of our baby.

My motivation for getting married was not so much about love as it was about me wanting to be a part of my child's life, no matter what. I didn't want to be a part-time dad. I wanted to be fully present in my child's life, and I wanted him or her to have my surname, and if this meant me getting married, then so be it. I did not grow up envisioning myself as a married man. Marriage was certainly not something I aspired to. Marriage was not something I thought about deeply or prayed for or even wished for. So much had happened between Elrees and me that love honestly had nothing to do with it. I was just determined to be a responsible, present dad. Elrees fell pregnant and that was that.

I wonder if my father was also in the same situation all those years back when he first became a father. I wonder if his overriding motivation in getting married was love or if it was about taking responsibility for his actions. My mother swears that they were both very much in love when she fell pregnant and that they were going to get married anyway.

They say the honeymoon – the butterflies in the stomach – phase dies down after about six months to a year, and any action after that is driven by one's resolve and not so much by one's feelings. I was way past the honeymoon and the butterflies-in-the-stomach phase and was purely driven by logic, which was to get married to the woman that I had impregnated. I did not want to have children with different women. I wanted all my children to have the same surname and to be born of the same mother, in the same way that I grew up. That was the logical thing to do. I know that it's not romantic at all and no woman wants to hear that, but my decision to get married was really based on what was logical and had little to do with love.

Yes, I loved her, but to be honest at this point, more than anything, we were managing the consequences of our actions during our grieving period. Everything was happening so fast. It was one thing after another. We were in constant crisis-management mode. The South African government is often criticised for being reactive whenever a crisis occurs, because of a lack of proatctive planning. I can say that we were just like the South African government, because of our failure to plan. We didn't sit down and plan any of this. We had made choices purely out of emotion, and now we were managing the consequences. There was no proper planning and foresight. We didn't talk extensively, for example, about where we were planning to live together. What kind of house? What kind of school was our child going to attend? How were we going to work with our finances? This pattern unfortunately would characterise our marriage negatively for a long time to come. We both came from divorced homes, both carrying our own fractured experiences, and we were just forging ahead the best way we knew how.

After that weekend Elrees returned to Kimberley, where she immediately resigned from her job, thus abandoning her CCMA process as well. She came back to Johannesburg, where I was to look after her and the baby. It was a move that was welcomed by both families. I used the 'marriage' letter that had been signed by both our families to get Elrees on my medical aid, and because she had been on the same scheme before there was no problem transferring her to mine with immediate effect. I was so thankful, especially given her kidney stone situation.

The initial plan was that she was to move in with me at my place in Brakpan, but because of her health scares she wanted to be closer to the hospital, to her gynaecologist Dr van Tonder and to her family. So we moved to her flat instead.

It was not an easy move for me at all. It was a period of great adjustment. My car was in arrears and the bank was threatening to repossess it. I had a pregnant, unemployed wife to look after and I had to take care of her home-loan repayments as well. To avoid the embarrassment of having the repo people come over to take it away from me forcibly, I handed my vehicle back to the bank and I reverted to using my old beat-up Bon Jovi. I got a tenant for my house and I moved in with Elrees.

The pregnancy was not an easy one. Elrees was in discomfort most of the time, mostly due to her kidney stone. But her regular antenatal appointments reassured us that everything was on track. This time around, we made a promise that we were not going to find out the baby's sex until after it was born, and luckily for us the scans didn't reveal much. Elrees was convinced that it was a girl, while I didn't care much. I just wanted a healthy baby this time, that's all.

But one night I had a dream about the baby. I could see its face clearly. It had big eyes and big cheeks and it was fair in complexion with thick, curly hair. It looked me straight in the eyes and smiled at me. It was a boy. When I woke up I was filled with joy and I couldn't wait to finally meet him. I told Elrees about the dream, but she was adamant that it was a girl.

On 2 October 2009, about a month before the baby was due, I went to work as normal. It was a Friday. I was looking forward to a chilled evening with a six-pack or two of beers when I came back home. Elrees asked if I could go past the Oriental Plaza after work to get her something. I can't recall what exactly. Maybe it was a mommy overnight bag. In my mind I thought that we still had time to do the last-minute shopping for the baby. Her friends and family were planning a baby shower.

But at around three in the afternoon, just as I was about to leave work, she called to tell me that she was in pain. The baby was moving non-stop. I abandoned the Oriental Plaza errand and rushed home. When I got there, she had already packed a bag for herself and we drove straight to the hospital. Initially we both thought that it was probably the kidney stone acting up. We arrived at the emergency reception area at around 17:30. The nurse who received us and checked her told us without a shadow of doubt that the baby was coming. We were stunned.

'But I still have a few more weeks,' Elrees told the nurse.

'Unfortunately, it's not up to you,' said the attending nurse with a smile. 'We have to prep you now for theatre.'

Neither of us was prepared for this.

'I told you we should've gone shopping for the essentials a month ago, but you didn't want to listen,' she scolded me as she was being wheeled to her room. In the room she called her mother with a list of items to bring to the hospital. At 18:30 a Dr van der Walt came in to see her. He told her that he was on standby for Dr van Tonder, who was on holiday. After losing Synové, Elrees wanted no one but Dr van Tonder to handle the delivery. He was in his late fifties and highly experienced. She trusted only him. She felt uneasy that someone else was now taking over from him. But there wasn't much she could do. The baby was on the way. Dr van der Walt assured her that everything was going to be fine and that it was all going to be over in no time.

When the nurse came back, she showed Elrees how to monitor the intervals of her contractions. At around 18:45 she was wheeled to theatre and I followed right behind her. I was given scrubs to wear, a hairnet and something to cover my shoes. I was briefed on where to stand at all times during the delivery, which was behind Elrees, just above her head. She held my hand and said a prayer. I had no thoughts of posting anything on social media this time around. I was fully present and in full agreement with her prayer.

I then spoke what I hoped would be some words of encouragement to her. 'By the way, the name I've decided on for the baby is Imani, which is Swahili for Faith,' I told her. 'It's a unisex name that can go both ways. I chose that name because I feel like after all we've been through, from losing Synové to now, the Lord has not forgotten us. That's why I feel like my faith has now been restored,' I told her.

'I like that. The name is fine with me,' she said with a smile.

By the time I looked up they had cut her stomach open. Then, in one swift move, the baby was pulled out of the womb and the umbilical cord was snipped. The doctor placed the baby on a separate table and immediately checked if everything was alright. I saw the bloodied placenta being sprayed down with water. I got a feeling of being inside a slaughterhouse. I turned back to the baby. It was covered in blood and afterbirth and was crying hysterically after being yanked out from months of slumber in its mother's womb.

They cleaned the baby up. I turned to Elrees and confirmed that it was a boy. Imani was a healthy baby at 2.57 kg. He was 51 cm tall and was born at exactly 19:05 that Friday evening. He looked exactly as I had seen him in my dream. I was now a father and I had this beautiful, healthy, living soul to show for it.

18

Making a home

Imani's arrival brought a lot of changes in our lives. Although he was a healthy baby he had terrible colic that would give us many sleepless nights. I could still go to work and get a bit of a break. But this was not the case for Elrees, who was with the baby 24 hours a day, seven days a week. She was tired. She was miserable. She still had the kidney stone to contend with, and no matter what she tried she just couldn't produce enough breast milk for Imani. She was a new mother and wanted everything to be perfect. The nightmare of losing Synové was still very fresh in her mind and heart, and so she didn't want anything to go wrong with Imani.

I would come home from work, eat an already prepared meal, play with my son, rub out some winds, make him burp and then go out to the balcony for a cigarette. Elrees hated how insensitive I was about the smoking.

'But I'm smoking outside,' I would tell her.

'Even if you smoke outside, the smoke still sticks to your clothes, and it affects the baby when you come inside,' she would tell me, and it did. A couple of months later Imani was in hospital for three days with bronchitis which had been brought on by the smoking, amongst other factors. But I continued smoking every chance I got. I was stubborn. I was shouldering most of the financial responsibilities and so I felt I should be allowed to indulge in a cigarette or two at least.

On weekends I would drink my beer, lie on the couch and watch movies or sports to my heart's content.

'How is it that you can just sit around and do nothing to help around here?' she would start.

'I work,' I would defend myself.

'And what do I do? Just sit around all day?' she would hit back. 'Tumi, I am tired. I am exhausted. I must look after the baby and I must cook and clean around here. Why? Because I'm the woman? The flat is a mess, and you're not doing anything to help, and on top of that you still have the audacity to ask me for some at night. You are such a sexist and chauvinist bastard, you know that? A real stubborn Pedi man.'

Physically she was changing also. Her hair was falling out and she was getting black spots on her body. Her hormones were re-aligning, I figured. She was frustrated on all fronts.

'So what do you want me to do?' I would ask her.

'I don't know – cook, clean, do the laundry, hold the baby while I get some sleep, or wake up at night to be with the baby. I don't know. Take your pick.'

It wasn't really fair for her to suggest that I was doing nothing at all. I could've done better, yes. I could've helped out more. The suggestion that I was not doing anything at all was simply not true. But it was her truth.

'I want a helper,' she said to me one day.

'My mother raised us without a helper so why do you need one?' I asked her, dismissively.

'I'm not your mother and we are going to get a helper,' she affirmed. 'Washing dishes and cooking only once in a blue moon and expecting credit for it is just not going to cut it any more. I want more effort from your side in the running of the household and I want more hands to help with the baby as well,' she said.

I felt like she was just being lazy. But every day she would complain about it. So I finally agreed.

We struggled to find a good helper. The first one we got didn't last for more than two days. A close family friend had recommended her. She was from Mahikeng and she came to us by taxi. On her way I kept making contact with her. Sometimes she would answer and sometimes she wouldn't, and sometimes when she did answer she would sound completely oblivious to what we had just talked about earlier. We kept miscommunicating on the phone and because of that a feeling of mistrust came over me. I had heard countless horror stories of babies being snatched away by their sitters and I couldn't take that chance with my newborn baby Imani. I had a strong feeling that the person on the phone was not the same person I had initially communicated with, but I could not tell her not to come any more because she was already on a taxi.

She arrived late at night. We offered her food and a place to sleep in the next room. In the morning I left for work. When I came back in the afternoon I found that Elrees had left Imani with this stranger of a woman from Mahikeng. I kept calling her on her phone but to no avail. Finally, when it was getting dark outside, she answered her phone. She told me that she was on her way back home. She had been to a urologist in Krugersdorp, the best one in town apparently, to consult about her kidney stone.

'I couldn't miss this appointment, Tumi, and so I had no choice but to leave Imani with the new babysitter,' she said.

But I was fuming. That night we had one of our worst fights.

In the morning I told this lady from Mahikeng that unfortunately we could not keep her because I honestly didn't trust her. I gave her taxi fare and then she left. She was very unimpressed with us and how we had treated her.

Elrees then arranged for her cousin Natasha to come over every day to help. I would fetch her from the bus stop every morning and drop her at the flat before driving to work. The arrangement worked. Natasha helped a great deal in steadying the ship. But I felt like this ship was heading towards an iceberg one way or another.

I had thought that if I did right by Elrees by taking out *magadi* for her, and by just being there for her and the baby, then my job would be complete. But she was not content at all. She was always uneasy and always anxious. Her spirit was forever restless. Something was always missing. Maybe I had underestimated how much losing Synové, as well as her bad work experience in Kimberley, had affected her, but she just wasn't the same person that I had fallen in love with a few years before. There were hardly ever even moments, let alone prolonged spells, of peace in the house. Being a mother, something she had always wished and hoped for, didn't suddenly bring her to a place of deeper contentment. There was a big gap that she needed to fill, and I think subconsciously she probably felt that it was my duty as the man and the husband to fill it.

But I could do only so much, and, because I wasn't able to truly fulfil whatever it was that she was ultimately seeking, she ended up sparring with me at every turn. I was young and I was doing the best that I could. But she felt that it wasn't enough, and she would throw my efforts back in my face, sometimes overtly and sometimes not so overtly. So I developed some resentment towards her, at a subliminal level.

It would take me some time to realise that each of us, even though we were married, was still on the path of our own individual healing. At the same time, we were not playing home. We were making a home, and it was exceptionally hard, I must say.

———

On 3 March 2010 I received the unexpected phone call from my mother informing me of my father's sudden passing. He had only seen my son Imani on two occasions, and he and my mother had been planning on yet another visit. At the time we were making amends in our relationship, slowly but surely. We had been getting there.

I had been looking forward to a renewed and a more evolved relationship with my father. But then, with no warning at all, he was no longer there. I had been looking forward to the new dynamics in our relationship and how they would play themselves out now that I was a father myself. I had been looking forward to us, the three generations of the Mashaba men – me, Imani and my father – engaging in eye-opening conversations about life from our individual perspectives. Those conversations would never happen now. In the blink of an eye he was gone, and I was left to figure this whole fatherhood thing out on my own.

―

During his memorial service, held at the Faith Mission Church in Kwa-Thema, I heard stories of how the Grade Rs and Grade 1s at Sechaba Primary called him *Mkhulu* and how they loved him dearly.

Mr Sookane, who represented the parents in the school governing body, remembered how at every parent-teacher meeting my father would remind them to hug their children and spend time with them. '"Love them. Hug them. Spend time with them," was his usual mantra at those meetings,' he enthused.

Miss S Modisane, who was Sechaba's institutional development and support official, recalled how she had first met my father. 'As an IDSO, when you go to a new school there are all sorts of protocols that you have to follow. It's like you are going to see a king. It's a long journey and by the time you finally get to meet the king you've been introduced to so many people. In most schools you first have to go through the peer staff, the personal assistant and so forth, before you actually get to meet the principal. But when I went to Sechaba for the first time, Meneer Mashaba was actually the one who opened the gate for me. But I didn't know who he was at the time. "Heita! Hoezit!" he greeted, as he led me in. "*Ke sharp*," I responded. I told him that I was there to see the principal. He said, "No problem," and led me to his office. He offered me a seat and asked me, "How can I help you?" I was impressed by his casual and personable approach, and we immediately got to work fixing up the school.'

The current, and the first female, principal of Sechaba, Pearl

More, remembered how frustrated they would get as teachers at all the changes in the curriculum, and how my father used to encourage them: 'Do your job to the best of your abilities and don't worry so much about all these changes in the curriculum. Just know what you are here to do, which is to teach our children,' she quoted. 'He never made us feel like he was the principal. He talked to us like colleagues. He never let his principal role go to his head. He was our father, and he knew us so well. He knew that if one is like this then he will call them one side into his office and he would say "Talk, because I cannot allow you to go to your class like this."'

Humphrey Chiloane from the Kwa-Thema Principals' Forum recounted how cool-headed and humble my father was. 'As secretary of our principals' forum he always advised us against saying "MY school this and MY school that …" because it wasn't YOUR school but it was where YOU were working.' He said in my father's administration as a principal he was just as nimble-footed as he had been as a soccer player. 'He was never flat-footed.'

They were describing a side of my father that I had always yearned for, but never got the chance to fully know. The details of his life that I had used to pen his obituary now felt so linear, not truly reflective of the full life he had lived. It was during this memorial service that the desire to find out more about him, his life and the world that had shaped him was sparked. Little did I know then that this interest would force me to confront some of the difficult issues I had been carrying with me all along.

As I sat there in the front-row seats, listening to speaker after speaker, the physical image I had of my father was of a fairly young man, but one who was also slowly edging towards pensionable age. Gracefully so, nonetheless, even though the debilitating effects of his diabetes had been clear in his later years. I can say that he was a man who still looked good and who still took good care of himself.

In our last few years together, whenever my father looked at me, it had been with a look of pride in his eyes. I secretly longed for more of his approval. The look in his eyes and his sheepish smile whenever I told him of my achievements, be it at work or when I told him of the first car or the first property that I had bought, had felt priceless.

When we met, we would never talk about the past. Instead, he was always encouraging, like when I told him that I was going back to school again to try out for a second degree, even though I failed at that attempt.

'I'm also studying through the University of Johannesburg. Education never stops. Keep pressing,' he told me.

Or he would make light fun of how big my belly was getting. 'You must gym, man. You mustn't have a *mkhaba* at your age,' he would tease. He also let go of most of the hatred he had held towards my mother. At the time the two of them were actually getting along quite famously. Everything seemed to be falling back into place.

The last time I had ever been really good with my father was when I was around five or six years old. I had no memory of us being good in my young adult years. I had really wanted things to be right between us again, and I was devastated that the chance was gone.

———

A year later Elrees and I moved into a new house, a stand-alone with a big yard for Imani to play in. I thought that this would be a fresh beginning for all of us. But the new house would actually serve as a stage for old demons. At the time, I was so caught up in everyday life that I didn't give myself enough time to process or to reflect on the losses – first my daughter, now my father – that had happened in quick succession. Everything was moving so fast. I didn't have time to pause and to properly grieve, and I think it was then that the 'strange man' within arose.

I had always been a very cool and loving father towards my son Imani back at the flat. I used to love hanging out with him, especially on weekends. Elrees had started working again, and sometimes she would work on weekends. So weekends were mostly our time, Imani's and mine. I used to spend a lot of time with him. Taking videos and pictures of him. Feeding him and putting him to sleep. He was the most adorable creature I had ever seen. I used to love rolling around on the floor with him while he learnt how to crawl.

But in this new house something changed significantly in our relationship, something horrifyingly similar to how my relationship with my father first changed. It was when Imani was was starting to come into his own as a human being. I think he was now two going on three. He was a happy and a playful child, though one who always needed some reassurance. But something inside me just could not accept that about him. I saw him, at that young age, as an unthinking, bumbling fool. It was as if I just couldn't stand the happy-go-lucky air that he had, and I wanted to take that joy away from him. I also saw him as someone who was very unsure of himself, who always needed affirmation, who was not independent but needed a guiding hand. I felt that surely such a person could never make it in this cruel and harsh world.

He was still very young. He was still formulating his personality. He was still coming into in his own, but something inside me kept pushing me to get him 'right'. I don't know why but I was eager to straighten him out fast. It was as if my time was running out.

I was seeking my voice as a new father, and strangely, the voice that I assumed was that of my father when he was also a young man. His parenting approach at that stage had been strict, heavy-handed and psychologically abusive, and it's ironic how I, having been the one on the receiving end of that kind of parenting, was now mimicking that very same approach.

I was exceptionally hard on him, especially during his potty-training phase. When I was alone with him I would shout at him if he had an accident. I would get irritated when I had to change him and clean him up and I would whack him on his buttocks, thighs and back. One day I slapped him so hard on the side of his back that I left a reddened five-finger print mark.

Elrees noticed it when she was giving him a bath in the evening.

'Come with me to the bathroom, please. I want to show you something,' she said. She was very disturbed.

Imani was in the bathtub splashing the water about and having the time of his life. Elrees grabbed his arm and her eyes directed me to look at his backside which had the imprint of my open hand branded on it. I was horrified, and ashamed of what I saw.

'Please stop it,' she said, close to tears. She didn't blow her lid or anything like that. She was calm. But she was very disturbed in her spirit. I had crossed the line.

'It won't happen again,' I promised her.

He was still a toddler and there I was unleashing the same kind of fury on him as my father once did on me. I was the 'strange man' now.

I'd say my biggest problem at the time was alcohol. I was frustrated at life and alcohol was my temporary fix, even though I only drank on weekends. One could say that I was medicating my long-term grief instead of confronting it head-on and soberly.

I would drink and parent at the same time and I didn't see anything wrong with that. But it was a big problem, because I would be playful with him in the beginning as I was drinking and doing this and that around the house. At first, the alcohol would give me a euphoric vibe and I would tend to his needs and give him attention with no problem at all. But the more alcohol

I consumed the more irritable and short I would be. When I got to the stage where I had had too much to drink, I would want nothing more than to lie on the couch and watch sports. But Imani, the baby that he was, would still want attention, or he would cry for no particular reason. In my drunkenness I would get super-aggressive with him. 'Why can't you just be quiet?' I would shout at him, and then whack him to get him to quiet down. Out of fear of getting more spankings he would calm himself down and stay out of my way until his mother came home from work.

In my mind I was raising a man, and I thought that was the best way to do it, with tough love. But I was the one who was a bumbling fool really. The drunk fool who couldn't discern between discipline and punishment, between positive encouragement and breaking down a child's spirit.

My father never touched alcohol and I think that on some subconscious level I indulged in alcohol because I felt that it made me different to my father, that it somehow made me cool and relatable. But actually, I was not cool or relatable at all. I just couldn't parent without a glass of beer nearby on weekends.

'It's to help me relax after a long week,' I would say in my defence whenever Elrees raised the issue. But I was short-changing my son by giving him this version of myself.

I was at some level conscious of the wrong that I was doing, but I just couldn't control it. In my mind I knew that there was a better way to be a dad. I also knew that just because I was present it didn't mean that I was doing a good job. Imani needed a father who was sober both physically and emotionally, a father who faced up to his own past of abuse and who made it a point to not repeat the same mistakes that his father once made. But what I knew and what I did were ultimately two different things.

Sometimes I would just give him a dead stare and not say a word at all if he wanted something or if he had done something wrong. It was a loaded stare. I wanted to make him feel my displeasure by just looking at him. I wanted him to fear me without me even having to mouth a single word. When I lost it, inebriated as usual, my voice would make him wet his pants. He would pinch his member to try to hold it in. It was a stark reminder of exactly what I had been through myself.

I knew this in my spirit, but somehow I still couldn't do anything about it. I knew that I was doing something terribly wrong, that my behaviour was truly deplorable, but I just couldn't control this force that would come over me, especially when I had had one too many.

I was no longer as affectionate with him as I had been when we were still living at the flat. I hardly ever gave him praise. I could never just accept him as he was, to be honest. I just wanted to get him 'right'. I just couldn't love him as he was, and I think he felt that. He was a fragile child by nature, and I hurt his confidence and ultimately our relationship with my abuse. As a result, Imani would grow to be a very anxious child who was not sure of himself and who had little confidence.

Elrees and I would have endless fights about my parenting style. 'Read the book *The Heart of a Winner* by Pieter van Jaarsveld. It will really help you,' she would tell me. But I was stubborn, and I would keep repeating more or less the same mistakes that my father once committed. Even though I was exercising more restraint than he had, I was doing damage nonetheless.

While I was consumed with gaining a deeper understanding of my father and his past, in the present I was neglecting a future that was in need of my immediate attention: my son. My relationship with him would continue to seem all right on the surface, but it was uneasy on the inside for a long while to come.

―――

It was only in March of 2020 that I realised that something had to give. It was in the weeks leading up to the country's national lockdown as a result of the global Covid-19 pandemic. Imani's school had already begun phasing in online learning. He was now ten years old. I sat down with him one day at the dining room table to help him with his English homework. But I was pushy. At some point I even referred to his work as a 'disaster' or as 'disastrous'. Elrees, who was walking past, didn't take kindly to that, and she called me to order for being so hard on him. I defended myself by saying that I had also given him some praise during our homework session.

'You are so stubborn, and you're fucking up his confidence,' she stressed in her frustration.

'Watch how you talk to me!' I warned.

'I will talk to you in whichever way I want to, because you are destroying him, and I'm not going to just stand around any more, because he is my son too,' she said and walked out of the room.

I was angry and quiet for three days. But she was right. The truth hit home. I didn't like it at all, but I had to accept it. It was at that point that I decided to take my foot off the pedal a touch when it came to raising him, because I was actually doing more damage than good. I had to concede that I was being unreasonable in my quest to try to make him into something that he was not. I figured that the best way to parent him was to work on myself and to change who I was. That would be the best gift for him. I also figured that parenting does not always require one to parent as such. Sometimes it means letting go and letting things be. Sometimes parenting requires just that.

19

Neo
(A gift)

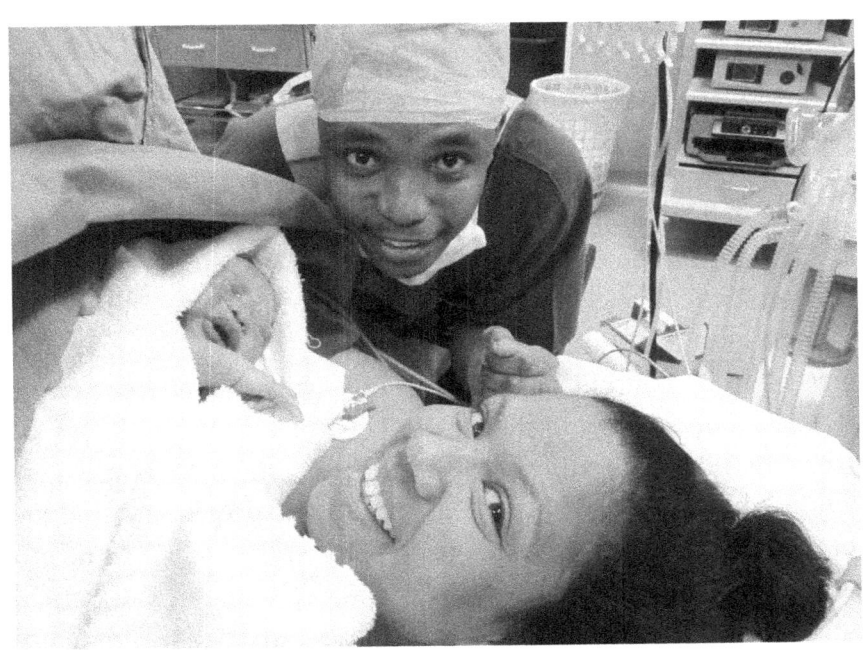

Right away after our 'white wedding', on 27 November 2011, an occasion that Elrees had been longing for, we started working on baby number two.

We took a deliberate decision to fall pregnant this time around. For the first couple of months that we tried, nothing happened. We then consulted with Dr van der Walt, the gynaecologist who had successfully delivered Imani.

'There's nothing wrong,' he told us. 'How often is your frequency in the bedroom?'

'About twice a week,' Elrees said.

'You need to do more than that if we want to see results,' he smirked. 'The more you do it the better your chances.'

Elrees was now in her mid-thirties. Dr van der Walt told us that women of her age didn't usually fall pregnant in the first couple of tries, and that's why we needed to keep trying and to increase our frequency. It was the best news I had heard all day.

We tried again. We made sure that our coupling was in sync with her ovulation cycles and we put all the sexy lingerie that she had received for her bachelorette party to good use. When she was close to giving up and making peace with the thought that she might be a mother to only one child, she missed her period. It was around September of 2012. She got a pregnancy test kit from the pharmacy and waited for me to come back home from work. When I arrived, she called me to the bedroom and told me of this development. She then peed on the test stick. It came out with two lines, which meant that it was positive. But she wanted to be extra sure. So she peed on a fresh test stick again, about 15 minutes later, with the same results. She was overjoyed, and relieved. She had been mindful of her age and also mindful of the age gap that she wanted to have between children. A four-year gap was a good number for her.

Instead of discarding the test sticks, she put them inside her memory box. Inside this box she kept the first pregnancy test stick from when she was pregnant with Synové; a piece of Synové's umbilical cord; the stent that was used to bypass the kidney stone; and the kidney stone itself, amongst other curious items. I suppose we all have our idiosyncrasies.

When we went back to see Dr van der Walt it was just to confirm what we already knew. Her pregnancy this time around would be much easier. She was now more mature. She was settled in her career as a news producer. She had a home, and a live-in helper. The horror of her past pregnancy was a faint memory, and I was slowly but surely making peace with Synové's and my father's passing. I thought to myself that whether the baby was a boy or a girl I would name it after my father, as a tribute to him. I was in a space where I was reading the Bible quite a lot and I was thinking deeply about lineage and legacy.

In marrying Elrees, I married a deeply religious, almost fanatical, Christian woman. Her influence over me should not be discounted – it is because of that very influence that I was now giving Christianity a second or a third try, reluctantly so. But on a personal level I was also looking for a deeper meaning in life. In this new stage of my journey I was watching my alcohol intake. I was also growing calmer and more loving. Elrees, understandably, liked this new version of me. I was pondering my existence in the bigger scheme of things and thinking about what my responsibility to the future generations ought to be. I had been through so much in my life and I felt like this baby was the rainbow after the floods. How right I would be. But the silent, awkward uneasiness between myself and my son Imani remained.

From conception to the final stages of the pregnancy, the baby was very kind to Elrees. She never gained much weight. Her feet and ankles didn't swell up. Her features remained relatively the same and she wasn't as sickly and as tired as she was during the other pregnancies. And the baby was just a delight. We even had a baby shower. We received lots of items like clothes, blankets and nappies, and Imani's cot was thankfully still intact.

The baby came on 9 May 2013, exactly as Dr van der Walt had scheduled. Everything was in place this time around, especially the mommy overnight bag.

The night before the birth, I fasted and I worshipped alone in my room. I wanted everything to go well with this delivery and I felt that nothing short of some spiritual uplifting and worshipping would do the trick.

In the morning we told Imani that we were going to fetch his little brother or sister at the hospital. Elrees had her mommy overnight bag in hand and she was ready to go. At the hospital they checked her in while I filled out some forms at the reception area. When it was time to go to theatre I was briefed on the drill by one of the attending nurses. By now I was pretty much clued up about the dos and don'ts. Elrees and I were both calmer and more relaxed. Experience is indeed the best teacher, I thought. I prided myself on having been physically present in the delivery room for all of my children. In theatre I was handed some protective wear to cover my hair, upper body and shoes and I was shown where to stand. I had a small digital camera with fresh batteries. I took some snaps while Elrees was being prepped. Dr Tshigabe, the paediatrician, then casually walked in. Cool and calm. From the look on Dr van der Walt's face I could tell that he was not impressed by the timing of his arrival. But Dr Tshigabe was unfazed. Inside that theatre they were both equals and there was nothing Dr van der Walt could say or do but just make peace with it. Elrees held my hand and said a prayer as they were cutting her open, her third caesarean section. In one swift move they pulled the baby out.

It was a girl. Elrees had been hoping and praying for a baby girl. Neo, as I would name her, was the perfect gift. She cried so much as they pulled her out. She was red with blood. She had fat cheeks and her upper lip was protruding slightly. She kept her eyes shut tight as Dr Tshigabe checked her. Elrees asked me why she was crying so much. I told her that she was fine.

'They are just cleaning her up,' I told her. She was a big baby too. She came in at 3 kg and she was 50 cm tall. The nurses gave her to Elrees to hold her. The anaesthetist asked if she could take a snap of the three of us. I gave her my camera and we got a beautiful photo out of that moment.

Imani was waiting outside in the reception area with his granny Gloria. I came out to tell them that all had gone well.

'Can I go in to have a look at my baby sister, Daddy?' asked Imani.

'You can only see her at night during visiting hours through the glass window,' I told him with a chuckle. He was a little disappointed.

I went back to check up on Elrees. She was out cold. I grabbed a chair and sat by her bedside. I sent some baby pics to family members on my phone. When Elrees came to, her throat was dry. She was in pain. But it was a familiar kind of pain. She had been butchered and stitched back up twice before.

'How's the baby?' she asked.

'She's fine,' I told her. I could tell that she was happy. But she was too exhausted to show it.

When I showed her pictures of the baby she was concerned.

'But why is she so red? And why is her face so puffed up like that?' she asked.

'Babies are like that when they are born. She's fine. Ten toes and everything,' I assured her.

In the evening some family members came over to the hospital for a visit. Imani was cautiously happy at the sight of his new baby sister. He was still trying to make sense of what was happening, I suppose. Elrees recounted to everyone present how my maternal grandmother had once comforted her by telling her after we lost Synové that she would still have lots more babies. She no longer felt as if God was punishing her. Her heart was open and content and she was just living in the moment. The picture-perfect family that she had always longed for was now in place.

―――

Neo means 'gift' in Sesotho. I believe that God made her just for me in return for all the pain that I had to go through in life. She came into a complete world with two working professionals, a stable home and a nanny to look after her. Not to make the births of my other children less significant, Neo was indeed a planned baby. She would grow to be a much calmer child who spoke her mind and didn't give two hoots about my strictness or firmness. A thin, scrawny child with the biggest of mouths, just like her mother. I suppose baby girls do have that power to mellow one. It was because of her that I would see a patient, compassionate and loving side of myself as a parent. While my relationship with my son was not great, Neo would bring out a side of me that could be occasionally dismissed as normal, grumpy, old and boring around the house. Coming from the past that I come from, to now be labelled as normal, grumpy, old and boring by this little girl with a big mouth was actually pretty cool for me – a blessing actually.

I could not erase my negative treatment of Imani in his first few years, a treatment that would still pop out from time to time as he was growing into his own. I was not physical with him. But I would still have these bouts of me raising my voice at him, or being hard on him, for anything and everything. And maybe it was because he was the older one and a male child that I felt perhaps I needed to be much firmer and harder on him. It's a side of me that I'm honestly still grappling with to some extent. But with Neo I can see a positive picture of what I could potentially evolve into fully as a parent. Normal. Grumpy. Old. Boring.

Growing up, I always wondered what TV dad I was most likely to become like. There was no father or father figure that I looked up to or admired in any of the South African TV dramas and sitcoms. The portrayal of fathers or of black men in general was hardly ever fatherly. The Sesotho TV dramas *Matswakabele* and *Bophelo ke Semphekgo* portrayed black men largely as womanisers who fathered children all over the place and didn't take care of them. Magic Hlatshwayo in *Kwakhala Nyonini* portrayed a polygamist taxi owner who had a rural wife and a city wife but was hardly ever shown interacting lovingly with his children on screen. Ray Ntlokwana in *Velaphi* portrayed a stumbling fool and Joe Mafela as Sdumo on *S'gudi S'naysi* portrayed a backroom dweller who always came up with creative ways to get out of trouble. My humble assessment is that it was only when the first season of *Yizo Yizo* aired that we got to see some real father-and-son interactions, through the characters of Javas and his father. But I could be wrong.

On the other hand, I always looked up to and admired the dads that I saw on American-produced TV dramas and sitcoms. Initially the TV dad that I liked was Dr Huxtable from *The Cosby Show*. But I never saw much of myself in him, which is good thing, I suppose, in view of the revelations of sexual misconduct involving numerous women that have come to light. Then it was Tony Danza in *Who's the Boss*? He was a cool and youthful father figure, but I still didn't see much of myself in him or see me becoming like him one day. Another TV dad that I liked was Carl from *Family Ties*. But to be honest what I liked more than anything was the stable and warm family environment that he and his wife created on every episode. Then came Michael from *My*

Wife and Kids. Michael was a cool, tall, smooth and funny dad who I liked very much. He was a dad who always used to think up all these elaborate and entertaining ways to discipline or to guide his children, though sometimes his antics would get out of hand.

But when Andre from *Black-ish* came along I couldn't help but see myself in him. I could relate with 'Dre' more than any other TV dad I had ever encountered. He was rough around the edges, brutally honest, but a big, loving teddy bear on the inside. He was cool. But his kids didn't think so. They thought that he was embarrassing. They walked all over him. But he was not shy to say that he did in fact have a favourite amongst his children. He had a sharp, educated and a well-informed mind, and that's what I liked most about him. Representation matters a great deal, and I thought that we needed more Dres in this world, on and off the screen. He was this old, grumpy, normal and boring kind of dad that Neo seems to bring out of me so effortlessly, and I love this side of myself. Because of Neo I'm now working every day to make sure that this side of me becomes all of me and not just a part of me. She is my teacher and raising her is the lesson.

Epilogue

Papa, you were blessed with a stubborn spirit. But thankfully you were also blessed with a mind that was constantly willing to learn and to unlearn. What you got wrong with me and Tshepo, you certainly got right with Tumelo. You were a flawed human being like anybody else, but you were also a human being who was continually evolving into something better. A one-dimensional being you were certainly not. You were complex, Papa, hard to get, hard to read, hard to decipher and as a consequence hard to appreciate. You were never a ready-made father. There's no such thing anyway.

But as we came into our own, so did you in your role as a father. There were teething problems, sleepless nights, runny noses and heaving chests. You were there for all the doctors' appointments. When we crawled, you crawled with us. When we learnt to walk you were always at the ready to catch us when we fell, and when we learnt to run you were right there beside us. As we learnt from you, so did you from us. From your father, Tshungwane, you learnt how to be a provider and a disciplinarian. But through your own journey as a father in a changing world you also had to learn how to be a nurturer and a caregiver. You taught me the importance of a good foundation and why it should be in place from a child's formative years, because a good home is not something you can just forge later on in life when things are more convenient. It's something that you do now as life is happening. It cannot be postponed, just as a child's development and growth cannot be postponed.

It wasn't easy. You made mistakes, yes. But you were also present. In good times and bad you were present. Rain or shine you were present, and that really means a lot more to me than the mistakes you made as a father. By being present, you were able to make amends in the way you raised Tumelo. You never laid a finger on him. Instead, you showered him with nothing but positive affirmation from the day he was born. Today he is a headstrong young man, with a Master's in Psychology. Your being present alone allowed you that second chance. Your being present was central to our well-being and our emotional development. Your being present was a present.

In my short years as a father, I have found that fatherhood is a process and not an event. I've found that there is no one definitive answer to what fatherhood is and what fatherhood is not. I've found that it's about listening to your child's voice closely, so that you can hear even the things they are not saying. I've found that it's not wise or helpful to stress over finding your voice as a parent, as I did in the beginning, for that voice changes over time as you and your child grow. There isn't any one voice that is permanent. Tupac Shakur, for example put it so eloquently when he described his relationship with his mother thus: 'My mom's my homie. We went through our stages, you know, where first we was mother and son, then it was like drill sergeant and cadet, then it was dictator and little country. Then I moved out and I was on my own.'[9]

I've found that it's about providing exemplary guidance, for what they see they become. I've found that it's about being present at all times so you can have a relationship with your children, even when you do not have the means of providing for them. I've found that society will always judge you harshly for not being able to provide for your children. But I've also found that it's just as important to be present and active in all the other areas, because once that time is gone then it's gone forever. It's important to plan and to be fully conscious of one's decisions. It saves a lot of trouble and it spares the child any unnecessary hurt

---

9   Tupac said this in an interview, 'Tupac uncut and uncensored: The lost prison tapes'. Available at https://youtu.be/6jN-WeqToD4. (Accessed 9 June 2021)

and instability in the future. I've found that it's a two-way street where both sides learn from each other.

I've found that it's the greatest calling of all to be wholly responsible for a life that has its own soul, thoughts, feelings, ideas and imagination, and to be the vessel that helps it become the best it can be. I've found that it's about evolution, it's about understanding that the primary parenting and caregiving role is not only up to the mothers, aunts and grannies, for example, but also up to the fathers. Most importantly I've found that it's about continuously learning and unlearning and being able to forgive oneself in the process.

I've also found out that it's about doing the work you need to do to face up to your past, to heal from your scars, so that your children do not end up reliving your pain.

It's no secret how race and class relations during the apartheid years negatively shaped the face of fatherhood in South Africa. We know all too well how the migrant labour system, for example, disrupted all aspects of family life in South Africa, particularly for black people. But it's also up to us to not become slaves to our past. I've also found through this process of self-reflection that to change one's narrative one really needs to be the one who is holding the pen. Only then can we tell a better story of our lives.

About the author

Tumiso Mashaba grew up in a working-class family in Kwa-Thema, Ekurhuleni. He is a journalist, a writer and a producer who has contributed extensively to a number of news and current affairs programmes for the South African Broadcasting Corporation over the years. In 2011 he was awarded the United Nations Correspondents Association prize for a 24-minute documentary he produced called *Forging Utopia*, which looked at the repatriation process of refugees from Zambia to the Democratic Republic of the Congo. He is a bulletin writer for *The Globe* on SABC News (DStv channel 404) and a content producer for *Daily Thetha* (SABC 1). Tumiso currently holds a Bachelor of Technology in Journalism degree from Tshwane University of Technology. He is a husband and a father to two children.

www.ingramcontent.com/pod-product-compliance
Lightning Source LLC
Chambersburg PA
CBHW070840160426
43192CB00012B/2253